WOOD QUAY

The Clash over Dublin's Viking Past

WOOD QUAY

The Clash over Dublin's Viking Past

Thomas Farel Heffernan

UNIVERSITY OF TEXAS PRESS   AUSTIN

First edition, 1988

Requests for permission to reproduce material
from this work should be sent to:
Permissions
University of Texas Press
Box 7819
Austin, Texas 78713-7819

LIBRARY OF CONGRESS CATALOGING-IN-PUBLICATION DATA

Heffernan, Thomas Farel, 1933–
  Wood quay : the clash over Dublin's Viking past / by
Thomas Farel Heffernan.—1st ed.
    p. cm.
  Bibliography: p.
  Includes index.
  ISBN: 978-0-292-72977-3
    1. Wood Quay Site (Dublin, Dublin) 2. Northmen—
Ireland—Dublin (Dublin)—Antiquities. 3. Dublin
(Dublin)—Antiquities. 4. Ireland—Antiquities.
5. Excavations (Archaeology)—Ireland—Dublin
(Dublin) 6. Cultural property, Protection of—Ireland—
Dublin (Dublin)—Citizen participation. I. Title.
DA995.D9W664 1988
936.1'83—dc19   88-14309
                                                          CIP

CONTENTS

FOR JEFF

ACKNOWLEDGMENTS

AM DEEPLY GRATEFUL to the many people who helped me to gather material for this book; some of them are, in alphabetical order: Peter Addyman, John Bradley, Kevin Byrne, Matty Byrne, Noel Carroll, Neil Collins, Peter Danaher, David Davin-Power, George Eogan, Alexis Fitzgerald, Mary Flaherty, John Gallagher, Brooke Givot, Rev. Francis X. Glimm, Richard Haworth, Paddy Healy, Carmencita Hederman, Siobhan de hOir, Seamus and Celia Homan, Deirdre Kelly, Tom and Eleanor Kinsella, Shay Lattimore, Mary Lavin, Sean Dublin Bay Loftus, A. T. Lucas, Victor and Mary McBrien, Bryan McClelland, Colin McClelland, Margaret MacCurtain, Andrew McHugh, Rev. F. X. Martin OSA, Malachi Martin, Jean Mattson, Nicholas Maxwell, Kennedy Mawhinney, Carolyn Minionis, Kevin B. Nowlan, Michael O'Brien, Cecilie O'Flaherty, Eamonn O'Flaherty, Breandán Ó Ríordáin, Joseph Raftery, Mary Robinson, Rev. Finian Roche OFM, Bride Rosney, Patrick J. Russell, Etienne Rynne, Anngret Simms, Sam Stephenson, Leo Swan, John Vetter, Patrick Wallace, Dermot Walsh. If justice were done the most repeatedly generous of the above would appear in boldface, italics, and capitals. I've resigned myself to the injustice but still cannot fail to give special recognition to Bride Rosney, F. X. Martin, and Pat Wallace, whose help throughout the writing of this book was manifested in many kindnesses and in the answers to a multitude of questions, half of the answers anticipating the questions.

Among institutions that I would like to thank are the National Museum of Ireland, the Public Relations Department and the Development Department of Dublin Corporation, the photo library of the *Irish Times*, An Taisce, the Royal Society of Antiquaries of Ireland, An Foras Forbartha, and the Irish Architectural Archive.

NOTE ON IRISH GOVERNMENT

N IRELAND the word *government* by itself always refers to the state (i.e., national) government. The definition of *government* is the taoiseach (prime minister, pronounced tee-sheck) and cabinet ministers. The Oireachtas (Parliament) is made up of the Dáil (equivalent to British House of Commons or U.S. House of Representatives), the Seanad (Senate), and, technically, the president. The Dáil has much more power than the Seanad.

The local government of Dublin is known as the Dublin Corporation. All local governments in Ireland are overseen by a cabinet minister, the minister for the environment (formerly known as the minister for local government). The highest appointed official in the Corporation is the city manager, who is selected by a state body known as the Local Appointments Commission. The elected officials of Dublin are the members of the city council, who at the time of the Wood Quay controversy numbered forty-five and were elected from nine districts. In 1985 the council was enlarged to fifty-two members elected from twelve districts. The first person deemed elected in each district is given the title alderman; the others are referred to as councillors. The term of office of the council is five years, and its members annually elect one of their own number lord mayor.

INTRODUCTION: DUBLIN SURFACING

D
O YOU SEE those hoardings there?" Eamonn said. "That's Wood Quay. Have you heard of Wood Quay?" The car came up the hill of Nicholas Street toward Christ Church and turned right. Behind the cathedral, where legend puts the grave of Molly Malone and where in fact the earth has yielded bushels of her or someone else's cockle and mussel shells, I had a glimpse of a plywood wall running beside Christ Church to Fishamble Street and disappearing down Fishamble's curving hill. Across from the wall, midway down the hill, stood Kennan's Iron Works, a building which still shows the lineaments of a theater. It had been a theater, and Handel had been there April 13, 1742, for the first performance of *The Messiah*. About Molly Malone and Handel I learned later.

"No. What's Wood Quay?"

"It's a bloody national disgrace. That's what it is."

The visitor scanning a map of Dublin will find that Wood Quay is the name of a street running about two hundred yards along the south side of the river Liffey less than a mile west of O'Connell Bridge. The Dubliner, however, who hears Wood Quay mentioned today does not think of that stretch of street but rather of the four acres of land that lie south of the street between the river and Christ Church, of what was discovered there, and of the battle for the four acres which itself came to be known as "Wood Quay." Dubliners may or may not call it a bloody national disgrace, but they will call it something.

Wood Quay is the site on which was unearthed a major part of the original Viking settlement of Dublin; it is one of the major European archaeological discoveries of the century. The reaction to events at Wood Quay produced one of the most intense battles ever waged by the public to save any archaeological site anywhere. And Wood Quay became more than an archaeological issue; it became a political milestone for Ireland, a phenomenon that created more upheaval in local and national government and altered public thinking more than any cultural event in the nation's recent history.

Generations of historians knew that the Vikings had founded the city of Dublin in the middle of the ninth century, and they assumed that the original Viking landing had been made somewhere on the south bank of the Liffey. But that knowledge and those assumptions, although they were taught in textbooks and affirmed in the standard histories, were wrapped in the late morning haze which, until twenty or thirty years ago, hovered over Irish historiography (partly because submitting legends to verification seemed, first of all, among life's least urgent duties, and second, a bit unkind, like putting the old folks in a nursing home). When, however, Irish archaeologists began excavating the Wood Quay site in the 1960s the haze over old Dublin was dissipated and the Viking founders of the city were suddenly for real.

Under the four acres archaeologists from the National Museum of Ireland began unearthing in the 1960s the original Viking settlement in a remarkable state of preservation. "Remarkable state of preservation" means wood undecayed, cloth still supple, contents of stomachs of buried bodies intact, ashes undisturbed in hearths, coins in piggy banks, shoes just resoled, domestic furnishings, jewelry, toys, tools, artifacts, and houses and house plots mappable. It was a stunning discovery in the eyes of historians and scientists and the Irish people.

It all began with a chance discovery under Dublin Castle, down the street from Wood Quay, of medieval objects and parts of medieval houses. That discovery primed the pump. Within a year archaeologists were invited to excavate cleared land west of the castle and within another few years they were working on Winetavern Street, the street which borders the four-acre Wood Quay site on the west as Fishamble does on the east and a little alley called John's Lane, next to Christ Church, used to do on the south. By the time that work on Winetavern was started it was clear to scientist and nonscientist alike that early medieval Dublin had been found.

Excitement over the finds grew. While the Irish reacted with a natural curiosity about the new light on the beginning of their capital city, the first thing that scholars outside of Ireland reacted to was the new evidence that the site supplied of foreign trade and artistic influence between Ireland and the rest of the medieval world. It was well known that Dublin in its first three centuries was of little significance to the rest of Ireland but of considerable significance to the rest of the world, for the Vikings had made it an international trading center in communication with the network of continental and Asian Viking settlements.

Wood Quay, however, was not destined to remain a purely historical and scientific phenomenon; after a few years it became a political phenomenon as well. Before the archaeological excavations had started on the site, the Dublin Corporation, as the city government is called, had begun to clear the land of older buildings in preparation for the start of construction of a four-building complex designed to house the city's civic offices. It was, in fact, the initial clearance of the land that occasioned the corporation's invitation to the National Museum to come in and excavate until the actual construction work on the buildings began.

If what the archaeologists uncovered had not been of such importance, the good feeling that prevailed initially on all sides probably would have continued, a few nice artifacts would have been salted away in the museum, the archaeologists would have decamped for Wexford or Waterford or Limerick, the four office buildings would have sprung up, and the whole Wood Quay drama would not have been played out. But when the extent, variety, and significance of the archaeological material on the site became clear—and when the amount of time needed for adequate excavation began to be calculated—the four office buildings began to seem ominous.

The conflict was simple: down in the ground lay the original Viking town, the adequate excavation of which would take—there seemed to be a concerted effort to avoid using the word—years. Waiting to rise were the civic offices, the building of which had already been delayed for—there was no reluctance to use the word—years.

As this conflict became apparent, controversy over the use of the site broke out. Even as the archaeologists worked in the first Winetavern digs, bulldozers were operating across the site near Fishamble Street, not merely clearing the contemporary derelict buildings, but in places carving away the medieval habitation layers. Alarms were raised over the bulldozers' destruction of these parts of the medieval settlement; it added to the dismay that the bulldozing was being done not by a private developer but by the city of Dublin itself.

The bulldozers' enemies declared themselves. The "Save Wood Quay" forces surprised the corporation in some of the ways that the antiwar movement in America had surprised the Johnson administration: they grew fast and attracted a more varied membership than anyone would have expected; they were imaginative and original; they were relentless. Before Wood Quay if one had heard that 20,000 people had marched in the streets of Dublin, one would have assumed that it was a northern protest or a religious event. But not after September 23, 1978, when that number marched in protest against the abandonment of the Wood Quay site to the building of the civic offices; 20,000 means one out of every 50 Dubliners or one out of every 150 people in the republic. A protest of that magnitude over a cultural cause was, as far as anyone could remember, unprecedented in Ireland.

The people who rallied behind the archaeological effort did, in the end, save a large part of the Viking and post-Viking remains that otherwise would have been lost. Most, in fact, of what was saved would not have been saved without them. Foreign archaeologists observing the Wood Quay drama were struck by the popular and sustained militancy of the archaeological effort's defenders. Archaeology is a political science in all parts of the world, and conflicts over the use of sites are part of its daily business. At one moment officialdom may cherish archaeological work and fund it, at another moment dismiss and obstruct it. Private interests and public interests are sometimes threatened by it, and defenders come forward to oppose those interests, but there is a scale and proportion to the coming forward. Mobilizations like those at Wood Quay just do not happen.

While the Save Wood Quay movement was a partial victory, a compromise with the historical heritage and with science, it was also a display of power which took all the Irish, those who were happy about it and those who were not, by surprise. The struggle to save Viking Dublin transcended the archaeological issue and became a struggle against old habits and reflexes.

By the usual tests of representation, due process, and civil liberties, Ireland qualifies with ease as a democracy. But the rights that Bunreacht na hÉireann, the national constitution, guarantees, much of the populace subtly spurns. A women's rights movement, a consumers' rights movement, an anything's rights movement labors not so much against official opposition or special interest as against a widespread lack of faith in the power of the people. A democratic movement, thousands strong, whose resistance to the powers is enduring, resourceful, self-reliant, rational, unhysterical, and popular is a remarkable thing in Ireland. *Viking Dublin Exposed* is the droll title of a book recently published in Ireland about Wood Quay; the suggestion in the title is that more was learned—unearthed—about modern Dublin in the course of the Wood Quay controversy than about medieval Dublin. That may be correct.

1. BLACKPOOL AND WATLINGFORD

WHEN THE CURTAIN rose on Dublin archaeology in 1961, the setting was symbolic and auspicious—Dublin Castle. Originally built in the early thirteenth century on order of King John of England, it has had its moments on the stage of Irish history: Silken Thomas Fitzgerald besieging it in 1534, Red Hugh O'Donnell making his colorful escapes from it in 1591 and 1592, Robert Emmet setting out to capture it in 1803, and the insurgents of 1916 attacking it on Easter Monday. It is a quarter of a mile down Dame Street from Trinity College and the same distance in the opposite direction from Christ Church cathedral; it stands a bit back from the street, partly blocked from view by City Hall. It is one of the points of reference for visitors to the city, many of whom come to the upper courtyard to tour the lavish state apartments or to hunt ancestors in the records of the Genealogy Office, but the castle proper and the office buildings around its lower courtyard and garden are mainly used for unromantic administrative purposes, housing a variety of state and municipal offices.

For all of it merits as a historical center of the city, however, the castle was not a comfortable place for Dublin archaeology to begin: the area available for excavation was small, and the time of year was winter, one of those wet, chilling Irish winters which make the whole rest of the globe seem tropical.

The archaeology at the castle began with some accidental discoveries. Around 1960 the authorities in charge of maintaining the castle were concerned about the deteriorating condition of the cross-block, the wing closing off the east end of the upper courtyard, and concluded that the only safe course was to demolish the cross-block and rebuild it completely. The visitor today would have to be told that the wing is a reconstruction, so successfully was original detail matched. In October 1961 the demolition of the old cross-block was completed. The excavation of the foundations uncovered pieces of glazed medieval pottery and ash heaps, meat bones, sea shells, and other signs of early habitation; it also uncovered an early foundation wall tentatively identified as the very first wall of the castle built in 1228. The architect called in archaeologists from the National Parks and Monuments Branch of the Office of Public Works to study the historical material and to advise him on whether or not the uncovered medieval castle wall could be used as a foundation for the modern reconstructed wing.

As they dug, the archaeologists, working under the site director, Marcus O hEochaidhe, penetrated five "horizons" of undisturbed occupation layers containing material from the tenth to the thirteenth century. They found pottery enough to classify by style and they found jewelry, tools, and evidence of cooperage, spinning, and smelting. A comb that they unearthed contained the Ogham inscription "Ane," presumably the owner's name; what was most interesting about the comb was the fact that Ogham characters were used at all. (Ogham characters constituted an alphabet, apparently originating in the south of Ireland before the fifth century; the characters were lines and notches scored on a horizontal line and were well suited to the carving of inscriptions.) It was very rare for Ogham characters to be used on movable objects, and in all of Ireland only four such inscriptions had been found on movable objects. Most important, perhaps, was the discovery of parts of hearths, houses, and a plank paved street. Although the smallness of the excavations (a trench thirty-eight feet by eleven feet) made it hard to get much perspective on these remains, each of the finds took on special importance since they constituted the first real entry into medieval Dublin, at least the first entry so patiently and scientifically studied.

It was a glimpse through a window, but an exciting glimpse. Waiting for more than a thousand years to be discovered, old Dublin had turned into a kind of myth; actually seeing it had a jarring effect, like finding King Arthur's grave. Marcus O hEochaidhe wrote up a report for the Commissioners of Public Works which was quite duly scientific and descriptive but which could not help radiating a deep scholarly pleasure. Among other things, O hEochaidhe observed that for the first time a stratigraphic record was available which would establish a sequence of occupation for that part of Viking and Norman Dublin, that a fine collection of artifacts illustrating the way of life of Viking Dublin had been found in precise relation to the sequence of habitation, and that the house floors, hearths, and walls had been found fifteen feet below present ground level, making them the deepest deposit of occupation material ever found in Ireland.

It is natural to ask whether a thousand years had to go by before anyone thought of excavating for the original city and then only when it revealed itself by accident. In fact, the castle finds were not the first tip-offs that old Dublin was a dozen feet away waiting to be discovered. A Viking cemetery had been found in the nineteenth century in the Islandbridge-Kilmainham section of Dublin, an area that lay outside the city in the middle ages. And a more significant discovery had taken place between 1856 and 1859 just west of Dublin Castle: in the area of Christ Church Place, Nicholas Street, and Francis Street a number of bone combs, bronze pins, and other objects dating to the middle ages had been found when excavations were made for the laying of new sewers. Thomas Matthew Ray collected the objects found in the sewer excavations and recorded them in a diary, noting the depths at which they had been found. Ray's diary and the collection are now in the National Museum, as are a few other scattered nineteenth- and twentieth-century finds from various parts of the medieval city.

One of the reasons the nineteenth-century finds that Ray and others turned up never became much more than curiosities is that there was a reluctance until the digs of the 1960s got under way to believe that the area now recognized as medieval Dublin was really fit in the middle ages for extensive habitation. There was an assumption, based on the experiences of eighteenth-century builders and repeated in many writings on Dublin that the land was really a marshy bog; builders of two hundred years ago often had to sink deep piles in the soft earth before laying the foundations of houses. That soft earth, it turns out, was not soil at all but the accumulated moisture-trapping occupation debris of centuries, built up like drifted snow around the relics of earlier ages. The bog assumption was, historically, a very fuzzy and unreasonable one, for many of the features of the medieval city, like the later city walls, were known to have existed at locations that could be pinpointed even though no trace of them remained. City walls were obviously not built to enclose a marsh.

Another reason for the failure to excavate medieval Dublin, if the charges coming from certain quarters are true, is that Irish archaeologists as a group were absorbed in prehistory to the exclusion of interest in the middle ages. "The middle ages, that's just stuff out of the newspapers for them," a historian at University College Dublin wryly observed. George Eogan, who is professor of archaeology at UCD and head of the Knowth excavations in the Boyne Valley, firmly denies this; Eogan himself was a committed spokesman for the efforts to save Wood Quay both in his official capacity as head of

Ireland's National Monuments Advisory Council and in his work with other Wood Quay advocates. The late Ruaidhrí de Valera, a leading Irish archaeologist, was also a strong advocate of the Wood Quay work.

One may, in fact, ask not only why the known history of the city did not challenge the idea of the marshy bog, but why it did not by itself encourage archaeological investigation. The answer offered by several people involved in the Wood Quay effort is that Irish academics have always been document centered. F. X. Martin, a historian and later the most prominent figure in the effort to save Wood Quay, was one of those who felt that Irish historians settled too easily for paper research when they could have been doing actual physical research. "Edmund Curtis, the great historian," he said, "speculated once about what the city wall of Dublin must have looked like, but it never occurred to him that it was there to be found." Father Martin was even asked when testifying in a court case that arose out of Wood Quay why he, a historian, was interested in archaeology—as if history and archaeology were alien disciplines. (Because, he told the court, documents record major events, and archaeology reveals how people lived.)

Before the castle finds and subsequent archaeological discoveries were made, the history of Dublin and its Viking founders could be put together somewhat as follows. Ireland had been inhabited from mesolithic times by peoples whose identities remain a mystery despite the awesome passage graves and other monuments they left behind; it had been settled possibly in the third, certainly by the second, century B.C. by the Celts, who founded an elaborately structured, uncentralized cattle-raising society whose culture developed in a highly idiosyncratic fashion thanks partly to the island's freedom from Roman invasion. Dublin was not part of the Celtic scene, however, nor were any other towns, for the Celts were not town makers; at most they formed small settlements around monasteries, the so called proto-towns. For a thousand years this Ireland was the setting of the struggles between major kings like the Ui Neill of the north and the Eoganacht of the south and of thousands of lesser kings and their neighbors; it was also the setting in which the learning of the seventh and eighth centuries, which gained Ireland a European reputation, developed and flourished.

Then the outside world intruded. In 795 the island of Iona, lying between Scotland and Ireland, was attacked and plundered by seaborne raiders from the north. Iona was probably the most important and seminal monastery ever established in the British Isles; it was a pioneering center of learning and missionary activity from the time of its establishment by St. Columcille in 563 down to the time of its transplantation to Kells, where, scholars speculate, the beautiful book of scriptural illuminations was brought and completed. Nothing had prepared anyone in Ireland for the raiders from the sea.

It is not clear today what the name of the raiders, Vikings, or Vikingar, as they called themselves, meant, nor is it ultimately clear why in the middle of the eighth century the Scandinavian peoples awakened to the possibilities afforded by the sea and became explorers, settlers, and pirates. The Scandinavians had migrated and raided toward the south for centuries; their step up to lightning raids on foreign coastlines may have been the result of nothing but technology, their new achievements in shipbuilding. Ireland, Wales, England, the low countries, and France, were targets of the Vikings' early in-and-out raids. While, and probably before, the Norwegians and Danes were advancing to the west and the south, the Swedes were moving to the east. There is enough evidence to say that Novgorod and Kiev were Swedish settlements and that the Russian Vikings set up a busy trade along the Volga and as far away as Baghdad, where they had access to Persian, Chinese, and Indian goods—glass, silks, spices, and many more exotic items—which were carried back to their major trading towns. Once the Vikings had established themselves in North America (which they clearly did at L'Anse aux Meadows, pronounced Lancey Meadows, Newfoundland, and probably did in other settlements), their influence spanned half the northern hemisphere.

The earliest recorded Viking raid on the British Isles was on the monastery island of Lindisfarne in 793. The next year there was a raid on another monastery, probably Jarrow, and then in 795 an attack on Lambay Island near present-day Dublin and, as noted, Iona. In 799 the Vikings attacked the coast of Aquitaine. Two other attacks on Iona followed the 795 raid, one in 802 and another in 806; the latter, in which sixty-eight monks died, led to the move to the inland Irish site of Kells. Frequent coastal raids continued for about half a century.

The Vikings arrived at Dublin by stages. They raided Howth, which today is part of the city of Dublin, in 821. In 827 they were a few miles south of this point at the mouth of the Liffey, and ten years after that they sailed up the Liffey. When one puts these desultory contacts alongside the activity of the Vikings in the north, where under their leader Turgeis they were ravaging Loch Neagh, Meath, and Connacht, it seems that the Liffey estuary was at first less appealing to them than other parts of Ireland.

The Vikings' landing at what was to become their Dublin base was in 837, but the Viking settlement of Dublin is usually dated from 841, for that was the year that the Vikings built a longphort there: in a longphort ships were drawn up on land and a fortified wall built around them. The selection of Dublin as a site for settlement may be a sign that after years of exploring the Irish coast the Vikings had finally concluded that Dublin was a superior location; the growth of the settlement was rapid.

From their earliest years the Vikings seem to have had some dealings other than plundering with the local Irish. What Irish? Were there any Irish people at all living in the area where the Vikings settled or were the Vikings the unqualified founders of Dublin? The traditional view that the Celts had no towns is taken to mean a priori that the Celts had no Dublin.

This view is still acceptable in many up-to-date Irish academic circles. It is probably safe to say that it is held by most of the academics and scientists connected with the Dublin archaeological excavations. It is certainly the view of Pat Wallace, the director of the Wood Quay excavations.

But there is a revisionist school that would situate a tangible Irish community on the spot, a pre-Viking Dublin. The leading exponents of this view are Anngret Simms, of the geography department of University College Dublin, and Howard Clarke of UCD's medieval history department.

There is no question that there are references to the site of present-day Dublin before the arrival of the Vikings and that two different parts of that site had names. One of the names was Baile Átha Cliath or Town of the Ford of the Wattles. It referred to the Liffey crossing, which was constructed early enough to be mentioned by Adomnán in his seventh-century life of Columcille and situated probably in the vicinity of today's Bridge Street and the Four Courts. The crossing was probably a heavy raft-like structure woven from wattles and spanning the then wider and shallower river. Whether or not there were settlers around the bridge, say, a group of fishermen, is a matter of speculation. The name Baile Átha Cliath (or simply Áth Cliath) is the present Irish name of Dublin; one meets it on postmarks, road signs, and official documents.

The other part of the site to have a name was Dubh Linn, the dark pool, presumably the tidal pool created at the point where the river Poddle entered the Liffey. This would have been a little less than half a mile east of the ford site, roughly where the garden of Dublin Castle lies today. (In the ninth century the Liffey was much wider than it is today and came up to the hill where the castle was later built.) The Vikings learned the name of this site and took it as the name of their settlement. If Dubh Linn had a population, it may have been monastic; nothing is known of such a settlement, but there is speculation that one preceded the medieval parish of St. Peter's, whose boundaries are suggested by a peculiarly curving present-day pattern of streets in the area.

So there were two places, whatever they amounted to, already recognized before the Vikings camped on them—Watlingford and Blackpool if their names had been anglicized. If any positive evidence of Watlingfordians or Blackpudlians comes to light, it will prompt some new thinking about the city's origins and will probably be supportive of the theories of Simms and Clarke.

Anngret Simms is especially taken by the similarity between Viking Novgorod and Viking Dublin as well as the similarity between Dublin and Polish towns that underwent German colonization. In all these cases, she argues, there was no colonization by Romans, but there was colonization by non-Roman foreigners, and in all cases both natives and colonizers contributed to the development of the town. Dr. Simms does not think that the "black pool" settlement will turn out to have been substantial enough to justify counting Dublin among the monastic proto-towns, but she foresees a recognition of a greater Irish presence in early Dublin than has been allowed by most historians to date.

Regardless, however, of what the Gaels of Dubh Linn contributed, the Vikings were the main shapers of the city of Dublin. Their earliest settlement—or one of their earliest—was in the area of the castle or present-day Parliament Street, extending gradually west to the Wood Quay site and beyond. Streets quickly followed streets, business neighborhoods arose, and foreign trade brought into the new town products from other points on the far-flung Viking network. There had never been anything like it before in Ireland.

The Vikings were initially a curse to the Irish throughout the island. Blood continued to flow, churches were burned and plundered, and the people lived under the constant threat of being carried off in slavery. The Irish princess Melkorka, carried off by Norwegian slave traders at the age of fifteen and purchased as a servant by an Icelandic nobleman who made her the mother of a son, was thought by all among whom she lived to be mute until she was one day overheard talking to her child in a tongue unfamiliar in Iceland; it was out of shame at her fate, she confessed, that she had never spoken. Her story, which is told in the Icelandic Laxdaela saga, and which seems to be based on real events, had a more movie-like ending (her son escaped to Ireland and was identified as the king's heir) than most of the tragedies of abduction that the Vikings are credited with.

In Ireland as elsewhere the Viking has worn two faces. Many Irish schoolchildren in past generations were taught to see the Vikings as marauders and nothing else. A handful of politicians and others who were raised with this view were occasionally heard during the Wood Quay controversy asking, why save the remains of those pirates? The Viking's other face is that of the civilizer and artisan, the face seen by visitors to the recent traveling exhibition of Viking art or to the Gokstad ship in Oslo or to any of the major Viking restorations. Which is the real Viking? The answer, of course, is both.

One may observe several things neither in extenuation nor criticism of the record of the Vikings: even in their earliest years in Ireland they were sometimes allies of the native Irish; in Ireland as elsewhere they were assimilated with astonishing speed and completeness by the people whom they had invaded; whatever the extent of their ravages, the native Irish had done as bad or worse to each other and, on occasion, to the Vikings. If we are to believe the account in *Cogadh Gaedhel re Gallaibh* (*War of the Irish with the Foreigner*), a turgid but partially reliable history of the Viking troubles written in the twelfth century, Mathghamhain's destruction of the Vikings of Limerick matches any brutality that came from the other side. In an often cited article, "The Plundering and Burning of Churches in Ireland, 7th to 16th Centuries," A. T. Lucas, a central figure in the events at Wood Quay, concluded that between the seventh and twelfth centuries roughly as many plunderings and burnings of churches could be attributed to the Irish as to the Norse.

In 851 Dublin was overrun by new foreigners, Danes. They were just as much Vikings as their predecessors, but this was their first appearance in Dublin, for all Vikings in the settlement up to that time had been Norwegians. The Irish in their records distinguished between the Finnghaill ("blond foreigners," Norwegians) and the Dubhghaill ("black foreigners," Danes). Of all the countries invaded by the Vikings, Ireland was the only one with historians who noted the distinction.

For more than a century and a half from the date of their settlement of Dublin the Vikings battled with the Irish and each other in Dublin and elsewhere in Ireland, but the lines of confrontation were shifting and inconsistent: King Cearbhall of Leinster, for example, who brought Dublin under Irish control in 902, had been an ally of Ivar, the earlier Norwegian ruler of Dublin. Probably the most popularly remembered event from all of Dublin's Viking years is the confrontation between Mael Morda, king of Leinster, and Brian Boru, high king of Ireland leading the Munster forces, on April 23, 1014, in the battle of Clontarf. Today Clontarf is a middle-class residential area in the northeast part of Dublin, known outside of Ireland both for this battle and for a memorable scene in *A Portrait of the Artist as a Young Man*. The battle has been long regarded as the definitive conquest of the Vikings by the native Irish, but in fact the battle was between two Irish factions (Mael Morda had the help of Dublin Norse and some overseas Viking allies) and left the position of the Vikings in Dublin largely unchanged.

The century and a half that followed the battle of Clontarf was relatively peaceful and notably productive. There was a revival of learning in the monastic schools, new manuscripts were produced, and there were signs of a growing interest in Irish rather than Latin learning. Poets showed a new concern about their art, and a prescriptive grammar of the Irish language was in the making, the first such grammar for a western European language. This renaissance came four hundred years after Ireland's first golden age of learning in the seventh and eighth centuries, and even though it was native oriented, it happened side by side with the reception of new influences from abroad such as Romanesque and Gothic architecture and the new style of monasticism which St. Malachy imported in 1142 after being schooled in it by his friend St. Bernard of Clairvaux.

This is the period to which many of the Wood Quay finds are dated. An accurate view of eleventh- and twelfth-century Ireland would include not only its political history but the artistic and intellectual revival, which we now know much more about as a result of the discoveries at Wood Quay. It would also include the thriving commercial life of Dublin, which until the time of the Wood Quay excavations had to be inferred from records or extrapolated from what was known of the rest of the Viking world.

But the Vikings were not to have in Dublin a lasting city. In the second half of the twelfth century a figure came on the scene who permanently changed the status of the Dublin Vikings. Dermot MacMurrough or Diarmuid na nGall (Dermot of the Foreigners) has long been presented as Ireland's Benedict Arnold, although that appraisal is being challenged. He was a king of Leinster whose adventures unfolded in the following stages. Around 1156 MacMurrough supported Murtough MacLochlainn in his struggle against Rory O'Connor, king of Connacht, for control of the north. One of O'Connor's supporters was a certain Tiernan O'Rourke, whose wife Dervorgilla had been abducted by MacMurrough in 1152. When in 1166 O'Connor was finally victorious he punished MacMurrough for his opposition by confining him to a small area around his castle at Ferns in Wexford. But this was not punishment enough for the angered O'Rourke, who raised a force and attacked MacMurrough's castle, obliging MacMurrough to flee both castle and Ireland. The deposed king of Leinster turned for help to a source that no Irish king had petitioned before, the king of England. MacMurrough found Henry II in France, presented his request, and was given virtually everything he asked for.

With the aid of the Norman knights whom Henry had given him permission to recruit in Wales, the foremost of whom was Richard Fitzgilbert de Clare, better known as "Strongbow," MacMurrough was able after some reverses to land in Wexford and Waterford and to march on Dublin. A coalition made up of Vikings, Rory O'Connor, and O'Rourke fortified Dublin against the expected advance of Mac-Murrough and the Normans. In a maneuver more typical of later warfare, MacMurrough stayed off the main roads in his advance from the south and led his forces through the forests into Rathfarn-ham and on to Dublin from the southwest. Dublin was taken September 21, 1170. In 1171 MacMurrough died, leaving Strongbow his successor; part of MacMurrough's agreement with Strongbow was that Strongbow would have right of succession and that he would have MacMurrough's daughter Aoife for his wife. These conditions had been fulfilled, and in more battling that followed MacMur-rough's death Strongbow was able to secure his control of Dublin. Another historical dividing line had been crossed; with Strongbow Ireland passed into a fourth age: prehistoric Ireland, Gaelic Ireland, Viking Ireland, and Norman Ireland.

It was the Norman era that witnessed the development of Dublin as the capital of Ireland. Throughout the Viking years Dublin's role as an international trading center gave it a prominent place on the world map, but from the Norman years onward Dublin's role on the international scene diminished while its role in Irish life increased. Under the Normans Dublin became the administrative center of the country. The Normans were great rationalizers: what good is a country without a capital?

Both of the Dublins, Viking and Norman, had been sampled in the archaeological excavations at Dublin Castle. What was found there would not support exaggerated hypotheses, but as other excavations nearby succeeded the castle work, the archaeologists began to think that the little trench that Marcus O hEochaidhe had opened was not only representative of the medieval city but might have been the very heart of it. It was logical that the elevation that King John selected for his castle would have been earlier selected by the Vikings as the most defensible part of their settlement.

After the archaeologists had completed their excavations at the castle, the plans for the reconstructed cross-block were made to include a glassed-in viewing area on the north end of the lowest level of the cross-block. Behind the glass the visitor today can see the exposed foundations of the medieval castle and at the foot of the foundations—especially on days following heavy rains—the waters of the lost river Poddle, which now runs far underground and is visible nowhere else in the center city. The Poddle forms a little pool around the stones on almost the exact spot where it used to eddy in its *dubh linn*. Astonishingly for a place so dimly lit and far below ground, some green plants grow at the foot of the stonework.

Archaeological activity, most of it ultimately supported by the state, is so extensive in Ireland that one wonders how the small country's budget can manage it. An annual survey of archaeological excavations in Ireland indicated that in 1986 there were seventy-nine excavations in the Republic and Northern Ireland. Work on prehistoric remains alone involves a large body of scholars and scientists; sites which are accessible to the public are popular with Irish and foreign visitors, and their names are as widely known in Ireland as the names of national parks in the United States. Some treatments of Irish archaeology like Peter Harbison's *The Archaeology of Ireland* and E. Estyn Evans's *The Personality of Ireland: Habitat, Heritage, and History* not only give good accounts of the archaeological work throughout the island but are engrossing simply as introductions to Ireland's history.

Although some archaeological work, such as that at Knowth, is conducted by university archaeologists, the most widespread archaeological activity in the country is in the hands of the National Parks and Monuments Branch of the Office of Public Works, more popularly known as the Board of Works. This agency is charged with licensing archaeological work everywhere in the country, and its archaeologists oversee the country's national monuments, a body of sites that is constantly growing as cairns and crannogs are turned up or historic buildings made available in one place or another. It was the Board of Works that conducted the digs at Dublin Castle.

Such urban archaeology was a bit of a novelty in Ireland. Important digs are now under way in Waterford and Limerick, and on other urban sites, but the more familiar setting for Irish archaeology has long been in the middle of a cow pasture. If the finds in Dublin which followed the digs at the castle had been in a rural setting like that of the Viking trading center at Hedeby in Schleswig-Holstein, none of the political problems which Wood Quay produced would have arisen. Hedeby became in the late eighth century the chief

Scandinavian trading center during the Viking era. Hedeby's style and density of habitation, the kinds of crafts practiced there, its minting of coins, and the evidence of the volume of its trade correspond closely to what was eventually learned about Dublin from the Wood Quay excavations. But the modern town of Schleswig, the nearest to Hedeby, is situated a few miles from the medieval town, so that archaeologists who have been excavating Hedeby intermittently since the 1930s have the convenience of working in a rural setting and with undisturbed remains.

In any event the idea of excavating old Dublin had, since the castle finds, justified itself, and the trowels and paint brushes were not still for long. The next archaeological undertaking was continuous with the conclusion of work at Dublin Castle. On High Street, about four hundred yards west of the castle, the Dublin Corporation had cleared some land for development. The cleared land was on the triangle formed by High Street, Nicholas Street, and Back Lane, adjoining Tailors' Hall and diagonally across the street from Christ Church cathedral. It was also, as it happened, virtually on top of the nineteenth-century sewer excavations where the Ray Collection objects had been found.

Early in 1962, just weeks after the castle digs ended, the corporation made the cleared land available for archaeological excavation. This time the archaeologists invited to do the work were not from the Board of Works, but from the National Museum of Ireland. The choice seems to have attracted no attention at the time—no one, in fact, noticed until years later that the museum had not applied to the Board of Works for a license to excavate—but it was a choice that had consequences. All the Dublin excavations from this point on, that is, from 1962 to 1981, were in the hands of the National Museum, and the National Museum policy was, for all but the last two years of the excavations, in the hands of two successive directors of the museum, A. T. Lucas and Joseph Raftery. Around these two men the Wood Quay controversy swirled; as it developed they encountered a degree of bitter criticism and cutting accusation that politicians are, but museum directors are not, mentally prepared to treat as part of the job. One of them retaliated; one did not.

What the museum did in the nineteen years that followed its arrival on the scene was to conduct a series of four limited excavation campaigns and one massive one. Since there were interruptions in the work and progressive movements from one part of the largest site to another, the campaigns are variously defined and named, but in essence Dublin archaeology after the discoveries at the castle comes down to the following:

High Street One	1962–1963
High Street Two	1967–1972
Winetavern Street	1969–1973
Christ Church Place	1972–1976
Wood Quay	1974–1981

Breandán Ó Ríordáin, at the time assistant keeper of the Irish Antiquities Division of the National Museum, was director of all these digs except the last. Born on the island of Tawin near Clarenbridge in County Galway, Ó Ríordáin grew up speaking Irish, was educated by the Jesuits at St. Ignatius College, Galway, and later attended University College Galway, where he had his academic introduction to archaeology, a subject which had fascinated him since childhood when his schoolteacher father had shown him artifacts discovered in the countryside near their home. On leaving the university he taught in Dublin's Bolton Street College of Technology and Rathmines College of Commerce and in 1954 joined the museum's Antiquities Division, specializing in bronze age pottery studies. He was viewed all through the Wood Quay struggle by supporters of the archaeological effort as the person in the museum most favorable to the Wood Quay interests and most disposed to make changes in the museum. He was to become director of the National Museum in 1979. Despite the desk work in his career, he has a rugged, weathered look that suggests a life spent on excavations.

The teams of archaeological workers assembled for the successive digs varied in size from thirty or fewer on the early digs to more than a hundred at Wood Quay, and the workers varied widely in background. A number were archaeological majors from the universities, some came with special skills, some were wandering scholar types who had worked on other archaeological sites in various parts of the world, and some were workers with no experience in archaeology recruited from the unemployed at the labor exchange.

Perhaps the most knowledgeable person working under Breandán Ó Ríordáin was Patrick Healy, a sensitive, quiet man with training in archaeology (he had studied it as an undergraduate but never sat for his final exams) and a varied record of publications. He is also an artist and a poet. None of his formal qualifications, however, distinguished him among the archaeologists and others he worked with so much as his ability not merely to know but to embody medieval Dublin. He brings to mind C. S. Lewis's remark in his inaugural address at Cambridge that he would give a great deal to hear any ancient Greek talking about Greek tragedy—"He would know in his bones so much that we seek in vain." Richard Haworth, one of

Healy's colleagues in the Wood Quay cause, said simply, "He *is* medieval Dublin." Healy had worked with Breandán Ó Ríordáin on the Winetavern digs, followed him up to Christ Church Place, and then moved down to the digs on the Fishamble Street section of Wood Quay.

About the inexperienced workers hired for work on the site a lay person might feel a certain trepidation. Were the professionals ready to let the medieval remains be handled by people who were strangers to the theories as well as the techniques of excavation? Paddy Healy, speaking of these workers, said that at first the labor exchange tried to give them every wino they could not place elsewhere, and Breandán Ó Ríordáin had firmly to send back everyone who could not be trained. But many could be trained. Healy described, with intentional over-statement, some of those who worked under him as better archae-ologists than the archaeologists. One of the men from the labor ex-change, Patrick Appleby, had gained enough of a reputation as an excavator to be the subject of a feature article in a Dublin news-paper. "He was like a surgeon," Healy said of Appleby; "he refused to be hurried." It is a telling detail about the instruction of the work-ers that along with the principles of excavation they were given the cautionary advice not to jump up and down when they found some-thing important lest their movements disturb the find.

High Street One began around the end of April 1962. As the ex-cavators dug they found eight feet of ground that had been disturbed by the building of the eighteenth-century cellars, but below that six feet of undisturbed habitation levels. The soil through which the ex-cavators worked was the soft compost of the habitation debris, the presumed bogland of the Dublin histories. It was this excavation, working through the debris to the foundations of the medieval build-ings, which conclusively proved that Dublin was not built on a bog at all, but, originally at least, on boulder clay. One obvious inference from this discovery was that there was no reason to doubt that habi-tation remains could be found everywhere at approximately this level within the limits of the medieval city.

The excavators moved backward through five hundred years of Dublin history. There was nothing from the fifteenth, sixteenth, or seventeenth centuries, for those levels had been disrupted by the eighteenth-century construction work, but there was material from the fourteenth century and, as the layers were penetrated, each pre-ceding century to the tenth.

The area of the dig was not large, a little under five hundred square feet, but that was half again the size of the castle dig. The artifacts began to accumulate: a carved bone, a Viking bronze needle case, a gilt bronze brooch, a metal-casting mould, combs, leather, woven fabrics. Many of the artifacts, including the fabrics, were in an excellent state of preservation, a fact that usually surprises lay people. How could cloth survive centuries in the earth? (The excavators even found delicate hairnets in good condition.) The answer is that the soil was extremely moist and had kept the objects in it wet for centuries and therefore free from oxygen. One of the steps that had to be taken with many of the perishable items, especially wooden items, was to place them in water at once until they could be treated for preservation with polyethylene glycol. Even today many of the smaller finds are stored in water in the basement of the National Museum and larger ones in tanks in a facility the museum operates in County Offaly.

The High Street excavators found two houses measuring twenty-five feet by fifteen feet. They were one-story buildings with post-and-wattle walls and a stone-edged hearth in the middle of the floor. The houses had fence-like walls made by implanting upright posts in the ground at regular intervals and weaving reeds or wattles between them. This fabric of a wall was then daubed with mud to seal it. In the course of the next few years it became clear to the excavators that this post-and-wattle building was the classic Dublin Norse house. A few plank-wall buildings were found, but on all the digs the dominant architecture was post and wattle. On High Street as in the later house sites the walls of houses were never found standing; occasionally a complete fallen wall would be found serving as a foundation for a subsequent house, but in general the walls remained only to a height of about a foot and a half. The reason for this consistent pattern of razed walls was that the Viking houses were maintained only for a number of years and then replaced. The old house would be shaved to about a foot and a half of its foundations, for this was to be the new ground level, and on top of the old house a new structure would go up more or less reduplicating the features of the one it replaced. This replacement could go on generation after generation; the evidence of it is most easily studied in the house lots along Fishamble Street that were excavated in 1979 and 1980.

The first year's work at High Street One ended in November 1962. The students had gone back to class and there was no pressure to continue work during the cold months. In 1963 the excavators followed roughly the same calendar as the year before and continued their work on the same site with comparable success. Then ensued a four-year hiatus in Dublin archaeological work, which, however, did not seem to threaten the resumption of excavations in the future; the years off just meant that the museum was attending to its curatorial business and would be back on the site some time. F. X. Martin recalled stopping by the High Street site and thinking, how nice—we're in for years of valuable research here.

For several more years it was reasonable to think that way. In 1967 the corporation made more land on High Street available to the museum for excavation. The new site was just a few feet west of the first one and almost twice the size. Here at High Street Two the habitation layers, as would be expected, matched those at the earlier site. The excavators found a number of wooden vessels, textiles, bronze pins, pieces of ironwork, bone combs, and coins of Dublin minting from both the Viking and the Norman periods. (Dublin's first coinage was minted in the reign of Sitric Silkenbeard around the year 1000.) There were also some finds that amounted to links, albeit tenuous, with outside history: the lead seal from a letter of Pope Innocent III (1198–1216) to someone in Dublin (it was already known that Innocent III had addressed a number of letters on diocesan organization and other matters to Ireland), a seal matrix with the name of a west-of-England family, and tokens of pilgrimage to England and Rome.

The pottery fragments found on the site were glazed and unglazed, some Irish, some from Bristol and vicinity or the midlands, and some from northwest and southwest France. The French vessels especially seem to have had a connection with the wine trade from Bordeaux. Breandán Ó Ríordáin speculated that the pitchers and other vessels may have been bonuses offered along with the purchase of barrels of wine.

The most revealing finds on the High Street site were the remains of leatherwork and bone carving. A great quantity of worked leather, mainly shoes and knife sheaths, was discovered, as were deposits, several feet deep, of scrap leather. One common kind of scrap was the worn sole of a shoe, which suggested that it was standard procedure to repair shoes by cutting the stitching and replacing old soles with new ones. The signs that this area was the center of leather craft in Dublin supported historical records in which the area was referred to as the medieval leatherworkers' section. Today, standing on the High Street site, one looks across Back Lane to a sign on a building: "Samuel Parker, Ltd. 36–39 Back Lane. Wholesale Leather and Grindery Merchants. Wellingtons Etc." A little symbolic presence, as if the leatherworkers' guild had kept the site down through the centuries.

It also became clear that this was the section of the old town in which the bone-carving trades were centered. One hundred eighty examples of single-sided combs and a few double-sided ones were found in the eleventh-to-thirteenth-century levels. The material used for the combs was mainly deer antler, apparently shed antlers gathered in the countryside, for there were natural ruptures observable on most of the stockpiled antlers, and there was scarcely any evidence of other deer bones in the area. In addition to combs the bone carvers left handles, dice, game pieces, and trial pieces.

Some of the trial pieces, the practice work of the carvers, were especially significant from an artistic and historical point of view. Breandán Ó Ríordáin observed a number of similarities between designs found carved in bone on the site and designs familiar from old Irish metalwork and manuscript illumination. He compared one trial piece showing two semi-interlaced animals to one of the early panels of the shrine of the Cathach of Columcille made during the eleventh century in Kells. The style in both is that called by Norwegians Ringerike. In published accounts of his finds Ó Ríordáin has named several well-known Irish croziers, shrines, and manuscripts whose design resembles the work that came from the Dublin Viking workshops. So evident is the similarity of the Viking and old Celtic designs that a person with no impressions of Celtic art beyond those acquired from seeing the more frequently reproduced pages of old manuscripts would detect it. Even before the workshops of High Street Two were found, the excavators had turned up at High Street One a carved bone in the so-called Borre style (after artifacts found in a medieval royal cemetery south of Oslo) and a brooch in the Borre-Jellinge style. (Jellinge is a town in Denmark near which burial mounds have yielded carved treasure similar to the Borre work.) The archaeologists soon realized that future judgments about the relationship of Irish and Norse art, much written about already, would be contingent on what turned up in the Dublin excavations.

Near the hearth of a workshop on the site of High Street Two the excavation uncovered signs of metalworking—fragments of a crucible, slag heaps, and metal trial pieces. One hundred thirty bronze pins were found, some gilt, some silvered or tinned. Iron padlocks (with keys), belt buckles, knives, arrowheads, horseshoes, fish-hooks, and nails were also found. Breandán Ó Ríordáin enumerated many of these finds in a 1971 article in *Medieval Archaeology* and concluded that the area being excavated was unquestionably a major craft and manufacturing center in the early town. He also observed that the dating of the finds indicated that the Vikings had not all been driven across the Liffey by the Normans to Ostmantown (modern Oxmantown) after the Norman conquest of the city, as history books uniformly taught. Some of the artisans had obviously been allowed to stay on in Dublin.

While the High Street excavations were continuing, work on an additional site was started in 1969 about two hundred yards north of the High Street excavations. The new site lay across High Street and somewhat down the Winetavern Street hill behind Christ Church cathedral. Once again the land to be excavated was newly cleared by the corporation, this time for the construction of Dublin's new civic offices.

The area to be excavated on Winetavern was no larger than that at High Street, and work proceeded as on the two previous sites. The expectations of the archaeologists were formed by their discoveries on the earlier sites, and the occasional newspaper stories, most of which were solidly informative, treated Winetavern as a modest but interesting expansion of the museum's work. But the archaeological work along Winetavern Street was really the beginning of "Wood Quay," for the first digs there became in time contiguous with those that covered most of the Wood Quay site, and it was out of these that the fierce Wood Quay controversy arose.

Demolition of buildings by the corporation was still going on when the archaeologists moved into Winetavern Street in January 1969. The shops along Winetavern had been taken down from the south toward the river, where stood, at the corner, the jewel of the street, O'Meara's Irish House, a pub whose façade was a long tableau of Irish historical scenes executed with large, brightly painted relief figures extending around both the Wood Quay and Winetavern frontages of the building. (The figures were saved for the Guinness Museum.) Not only on the street but in the interior of the lot, where a hodgepodge of buildings of a great variety of ages stood, the demolition work was continuing. The little island of excavation that the museum had been granted was able to spread a bit as land became available, but the demolition took place on a steep slope of land and created some cliffs which it was not safe to excavate near. Nonetheless the finds began to appear as abundantly here as on High Street. The periods represented by the finds ranged from the ninth century to the thirteenth; again there was Irish, English, and French pottery, and there were bronze pins, iron objects, bone combs, and bone trial pieces. Although many combs were found, 230 to be precise, there was no evidence of comb manufacturing on this site as there had been on High Street. There was, however, such a concentration of lathe-turned wood objects, from handles to bowls, that the excavators concluded that the woodworking industry was situated in this part of town. More coins were found, bringing the total to date to thirty-eight, and on the lowest, the ninth-to-tenth-century levels, gold and bronze wire was unearthed. Among the more engaging finds were two small models of ships and two piggy banks made with the coin slot at the top and no way to get at the coins apart from breaking the bank.

Seeds found in a culvert that drained into the Liffey contributed, along with grain found elsewhere on the site and the contents of the stomach of one of the skeletons from the site, to some idea of the medieval diet. The early Dubliners ate strawberries, apples, cherries, plums, aloes, blackberries, rowan berries, hazel nuts, oats, wheat, barley, and apparently some grasses like goosefoot and knotgrass, which are usually animal fodder only. There was also evidence of meat and fish in the Viking diet. Fishamble Street, in fact, takes its name from the concentration there of fish merchants from as far back, apparently, as medieval times; the street was the fish-shambles.

Other finds, like a large number of insects found on Christ Church Place, shed more light on medieval health and sanitary conditions. After the last excavations ended in 1981, Pat Wallace, the chief archaeologist of the Wood Quay digs, said that once the collected data bearing on the health of the Hiberno-Norse and early Norman Dubliners is published more will be known about the epidemiology of their centuries than of any other period in Irish history down to the nineteenth century.

The Winetavern excavations were not all contiguous at first; they constituted four separate digs, although they were separated by only a few feet. The first dig was in the southwest corner of the cleared land and when completed looked like a backward L. The second was a small rectangle just to the north of the first; like the first dig it was worked from 1969 to 1971. The third dig was a long, thin strip in the northwest corner of the area paralleling Winetavern Street, and the fourth was a rectangular plot in the center of the other three. These last two were worked in 1972 and 1973.

The demolition of buildings on the lot continued near the archaeologists as they worked their sites. A red brick schoolhouse, an old deanery wall, one of the oldest tennis courts in Europe, another house, and remains of a government building that had been used as stables were cleared away. On the site of the old tennis court Breandán Ó Ríordáin made one of his first deep cuts. In another sampling on the same dig he found a wood-lined cess pit, a very careful bit of carpentry work, modern in fact in its techniques.

The cess pit contained a variety of interesting remains, as places of discard on old sites usually do. Another cess pit turned up at the corner of the dig, which was as promising as the first, but time and resources had to be rationed, and it was not studied at the time. Many of the finds on the site were merely located, noted, and covered over again until there should be an opportunity for full excavation. Although Ó Ríordáin had decided to postpone excavation of the second cess pit, he agreed to take some timbers from it to accommodate a scientist who was working with him. The scientist was Michael G. L. Baillie of the Paleoecology Laboratory at Queens University, Belfast, the British Isles' pioneer dendrochronologist.

Baillie's specialty was a useful one for the archaeologists, and the Dublin digs were a rich field for the dendrochronologist. Dendrochronology utilizes the varying widths in tree rings to date the trees. Since the variations are produced by the relative rainfalls of successive years, all trees of the same species growing in the same place at the same time will have identical ring patterns, and, since old wood can supply ring patterns that overlap other known ring patterns, an expanding pattern or chronology—even running through centuries—can be established which, once known, will permit instant accurate dating of any timber of the appropriate species falling anywhere in the same period and coming from the same meteorological area. Sometimes the dendrochronologist comes up with a "floating chronology," a group of ring patterns covering perhaps hundreds of years, ready to be matched with any new timber that comes along, but not anchored to any known year. Once a timber whose pattern has been taken can be identified as having been cut in such and such a year, the chronology ceases to be floating and becomes absolute. Then any new timber that comes along can not only be placed at its proper point in the sequence but can be given the date now known to correspond to that point.

Baillie explains that there was no dendrochronology at all in the British Isles before 1968. He began examining the possibility at that time of doing dendrochronological work and concluded after two years of investigation that resources for the study of tree rings were available. He set a long-range goal of establishing an Irish chronology that would cover eight thousand years. The potential of the excavations going on in Dublin was evident to him, and he became a collaborator on the High Street and Winetavern work. He discovered that there was a division in the kind of wood used that matched the Viking and Norman periods—ash was used from the tenth to the twelfth century, that is by the Vikings, and oak from the twelfth to the fourteenth century, that is, by the Normans. Unfortunately only the oak lent itself to dendrochronological measuring.

By the time he had finished, Baillie had dated fifteen timber structures at High Street and Winetavern. The dates that he assigned were informative for the archaeologists, while the archaeologists' data served as a control on his conclusions. On one occasion on High Street he dated the wood of a structure 1199; numismatic evidence on the site suggested the date 1201. The immediate result of Baillie's work at the two sites was a floating chronology that he knew belonged approximately to a ninth-to-fourteenth-century period but which he was not able to pin to any particular years. Finally in 1977 after he had left Dublin he found a matching pattern on some crannog timbers from the north of Ireland which were absolutely datable and was able to date his Dublin pattern 855 to 1306. He also established another Dublin pattern 1357–1556 which was confirmed by other evidence.

When Baillie asked Ó Ríordáin for samples of the Winetavern cess-pit timbers, Ó Ríordáin returned to the digging and supplied the timbers, but in the course of his excavation came upon one of the many surprises that the sites abounded in. Buried next to the pit was a bag of two thousand pewter coins or tokens. They were five-eighths of an inch in diameter and were stamped with eighteen different symbols. They were a total mystery. Unlike the three dozen coins found separately up to that time, there were no historical aids to identify them. Experts who have studied them speculate that they could have been illegal currency, counters designed for payment in taverns, or something altogether different which some subsequent discovery will explain. The find is unparalleled in the British Isles.

The most important find on the site in the eyes of many, and the one that was to attract the most popular attention, came in 1969, in the first few months of the Winetavern excavation. No one seems to remember who first saw it. Paddy Healy describes members of the team looking around the lot at the newly cleared ground next to their work area and noticing a row of stones just showing at the surface. They began clearing dirt from the stones and found that they were looking at the top of a wall. The wall turned out to be the original stone city wall built by the Vikings. It must have been preceded, all assumed, by wooden walls of some kind—the walls of the longphort or others like them—but it became clear as excavations continued that it was the city's first major wall and defined the "city limits" of a settlement that took itself very seriously. The wall is about fifteen feet high and five feet thick; it was not something built around a camp. The location of the wall in relation to already and subsequently unearthed residential and commercial plots explained much about the daily life of early Dublin.

Was the wall a complete surprise? Some students of the city's history had thought that there must have been an old wall of some dating somewhere in the area. One reason for thinking so is that a fragment of an old city wall, long recognized as such and containing the city's only remaining gate, stands just a few yards west of the Winetavern site paralleling Cook Street and built in a line that, if continued, would lead right across the Winetavern–Wood Quay site. Speculation about such a wall had appeared in the press after the Winetavern excavations had got under way. Paddy Healy in a November 1968 letter to several Dublin newspapers spoke about the likelihood of the wall being on the site but concluded, "Admittedly there is no record of the exact location of the wall in this area." And shortly before the find, Aedeen Madden, writing in the *Irish Times*, March 26, 1969, remarked that one feature of old Dublin "which it may be possible to recover is the city wall which would have run somewhere between Christ Church and the river." And so it did. The wall found on the site is in a direct line with the fragment of wall along Cook Street. There is a great difference in the two walls, however, for the one along Cook Street is of later medieval construction, while the one found on the Winetavern site is the original work of the Vikings exactly as they left it.

In this old part of Dublin the curious patterns of the streets, especially the smaller streets, are often explicable by medieval street and plot plans. This being so, it would be natural to project the city wall eastward from the Fishamble side of the Wood Quay site along Essex Street, but such a line would require a bend or curve in the wall at some point. As excavation of the wall proceeded eastward, the bend was found. Midway between Winetavern and Fishamble the wall turned fifty degrees to the north and then after a few feet forty-five degrees to the west again, creating a break in the line that came to be known as the "dog-leg." The wall thus arrived at Fishamble Street directly opposite the north side of Essex Street.

Even before the wall had been found, Sheila Carden, the secretary of the Dublin Civic Group, had written to the city manager in a letter of January 15, 1969:

> The members of the Dublin Civic Group are concerned about the whole future of the proposed site for the new civic offices. We feel that adequate time should be given for a thorough archaeological investigation of what is the central area of the historic city of Dublin, which has been an intensive settlement from earliest times of urban occupation. The massive scale of the buildings to be erected, combined with modern deep excavation methods,

will effectively prevent any investigation once the building commences.

The Dublin Civic Group, which was shortly to join the celebrated "Hume Street" protest to save some of Dublin's best Georgian architecture, was founded in 1966 to investigate and warn against threats to the city's historical heritage and general environment. It is presided over by Professor Kevin B. Nowlan of University College Dublin and has fewer than twenty members, who because of their expertise have frequently been called on as consultants and have gained the organization a respect disproportionate to its size. The group's letter is notable since some partisans of the civic offices later claimed that none of the defenders of the archaeological investigations had spoken up until it was too late. (The conservationist body, An Taisce, also objected to the planned development of the Wood Quay site but on aesthetic, not archaeological, grounds.)

An official of the Dublin Corporation's Development Department replied to the Dublin Civic Group that the corporation had been in touch with the museum and was offering it every opportunity to carry out any archaeological investigation or excavation it wanted to.

There was a fear among the archaeologists, however, which received no publicity, that valuable medieval material was already being lost. Paddy Healy described how he watched the demolition and leveling going on around him. There was no harm done near the river, since the clearing there was just to ground level, but as the demolition moved up the hill there was a tendency to cut lower into the ground and minimize the slope. The reduction of the grade by this deep leveling was so great that a high cliff face was left at the south end of the area.

In the summer of 1973 when the museum's work on the Winetavern site was in its last stages, the land clearance work by the contractors had moved to the southeast corner of the lot. Here, Healy said, was the largest removal of medieval material:

> They had the biggest JCB [mechanical excavator] that had ever been used in this country—three of its scoops would fill up a lorry, an earthmoving type lorry. If they had used a smaller excavator we could have watched what they were doing. I asked the machine operator if he could take off the brick rubble (about six feet on top) before going on to the black earth below so we could see what was in it. But not at all. He dug deep into the black stuff

and lifted it, and then all the bricks fell down in front so you couldn't see anything. Some of those fellows were very uncooperative. Just in the matter of a month that whole area was cleared.

July 25, 1973, was the last day of work on the Winetavern Street excavations. The site was abandoned to the clearance work, and the archaeologists moved to a new site that they had been offered. But on August 23 the clearance crews turned up some twelfth-century material on Winetavern. Paddy Healy describes what followed:

> Mr. Ó Ríordáin appealed to the Corpo. to have this material removed to a site where it could be later sifted for objects. It was agreed to stockpile this soil at a site near Chapelizod, where the Corporation had property.
>
> The arrangements were worked out in a very systematic way that would have resulted in all the rubble and brick going to the Corpo. dump and all the organic material being stored at a particular site which we shall call Site X. The way it was carried out was, however, a pantomime.
>
> The machine operator was instructed to load the rubble and brick into lorries to go to the Corpo. dump, and when he had exposed the organic material to load it into lorries for Site X. He made no attempt, however, to separate the two, but removed everything as he came to it, so that there was a mixture of both in every lorry. Those that had mostly organic material were then sent to Site X and those that had mostly rubble were sent to the Corpo. dump. The lorry drivers were all freelance hired carriers, paid by the load, and as Site X was nearer than the Corpo. dump, they nearly all headed there, no matter what their instructions were.
>
> After a few days it turned to rain, and as the Site X site was not paved the lorries were getting stuck in the mud. They then all headed for the Corpo. dump because they could get out of it quicker. Despite this breakdown in the system a large mound of material was eventually assembled at Site X. This operation lasted from 6–21 September.

Healy substituted "Site X" for the real name of the site in order not to advertise its location to scavengers with metal detectors, one of the plagues that constantly beset Irish archaeologists—and archaeologists in other parts of the world.

The new dig that the archaeologists had been offered was on the higher ground where the two High Street digs had been situated and lay about halfway between them and the castle. This dig, which began in 1972, was known as Christ Church Place after the street it fronted, a continuation of High Street. For about a year the museum operated Winetavern and Christ Church Place together, both under the direction of Breandán Ó Ríordáin. It was also in 1972 that work was completed on High Street Two.

The first finds on Christ Church Place were similar to those on other sites, especially High Street. There were some novel ones, however: a stone house built in the late thirteenth or early four-teenth century and destroyed soon after, and some inscribed objects including a very well crafted sheath. The most teasing inscribed object was a sword with a puzzling word on its blade: SINIMI∧INI∧IS. The word can be read backward and, by conversion of the strokes into N, M, V, W, or A, characters can be made to suggest a variety of phrases, none of them, so far, convincing decodings of the inscription.

The Christ Church Place dig went on until 1976. Its contribution to the total finds made on all the digs up to that time is extensive, as Breandán Ó Ríordáin reported in the *Proceedings* of the Seventh Viking Congress (held in Dublin, 1973; published in 1976) and of the Eighth Viking Congress (held in Aarhus, 1977, published in 1981). Since it was not on the Wood Quay site, however, but across the street from it, it never became part of the controversy, and has been overshadowed by both the magnitude of the finds and the battle of interests at Wood Quay.

In July 1973 the work on Winetavern stopped. Breandán Ó Ríordáin had told a meeting in October 1969 that when he started work on Winetavern he had been told by the corporation that he would have three months, but that he hoped that he would get more time. Obviously he had got it, but he was aware that much of what he had found at Winetavern was just a sampling, and that the great body of riches was still in the earth. No excavation would take place in the whole four-acre area between Fishamble and Winetavern until the following year.

The Wood Quay crisis which had been growing as by cell mitosis for a long time had now become large enough to be seen by the naked eye. Several naked eyes reported in the press, especially in the *Irish Times*, during the last year of the Winetavern Street excavations. Even unscientific observers could now see that the archaeological content of the Wood Quay site surpassed in density of finds and historical significance the expectations that scientist and non-scientist alike had entertained at the start of the work and raised the question whether, since no building had yet started, the construction of the civic offices on the site should be reconsidered.

Official views were stated in an early exchange of letters. On August 1, 1972, the Development Department of the corporation wrote to the director of the National Museum, A. T. Lucas, about the cessation of the archaeological work so that the corporation could commence work on the civic offices. Lucas replied on August 3, two days later:

> Many thanks for your letter of August 1. The main excavation at Winetavern Street was completed quite some time ago but we would very much like to test the stratification of the lower part of the site nearer the river. This could be expeditiously done by making a cut with a JCB and we hope to arrange for this in the near future. You can take it that the work will be completed by February 1, 1973.
>
> May I again express the thanks of the institution for the facilities so readily given in examining this particular site which proved so extraordinarily prolific in finds and information.

The deferential letter raises an obvious question: what did "completed" mean? It may have meant that the museum did not intend to do more, but it certainly could not mean that there was no more to do on this site "so extraordinarily prolific in finds and information."

When Lucas wrote his letter, there was anxiety about the archaeological site in a number of quarters and in the general public a kind of mystification. Just what was going on there? The onlooker, the just plain citizen, was predisposed to believe the museum. The museum was where the archaeologists were after all, and if they said that the work on the Wood Quay site was completed, why, that must mean that there was nothing more to do there. Wouldn't the museum be the primary defender of the archaeological work?

But all the pieces did not fit. Even at this stage the newspaper reports made it clear that there was every reason to hope to find the whole Viking village under Wood Quay. If that was true, why was work stopping? Maybe the corporation was so philistine as to destroy the whole find in order to get its new buildings built fast. Maybe something else was behind it all. It was hard to know how to react, but even at this stage letters to the editors of Dublin papers were calling for thorough excavation of the archaeological site and expressing anxiety about what seemed to be abandonment of the site.

Whatever unknowns were involved, there seemed to be four knowns: (1) the corporation would not entertain any idea of delaying work on its new offices; (2) the museum complied with the corporation's wishes; (3) the museum did not explain its actions to the public; (4) the only people speaking up in public for protection of the archaeological interests were non-archaeologists.

As events unfolded, these four interpretations of the Wood Quay situation became more and more substantiated, and it became easier to look upon the National Museum rather than the corporation as the villain in the piece. Intense criticism of the museum—"museum bashing," Joseph Raftery called it—began at this time, and mounted steadily for the next few years until both Lucas and Raftery left office and Breandán Ó Ríordáin took over the directorship of the museum.

Why the museum took the course it did and exposed itself to an avalanche of charges and reproaches which it was obliged to defend itself against almost without allies is a hard question to answer even at this date. The most conspiratorial explanation in circulation, and it is a popular one, is that a number of investors with close ties to the leadership of Fianna Fail ("Soldiers of Destiny"), the more powerful of Ireland's two main political parties, had secret interests in land in the area of Wood Quay and that they were intent on pushing up property values (something which the new civic offices would certainly do); their pressure on the national government and the Dublin Corporation to see that the office buildings were built at all costs led to the government, acting through the Department of Education, which funded the National Museum, pressuring the museum in turn to get out of the way and let the offices go up. While there is little hope of turning up the evidence needed to prove the charge in view of the secretiveness surrounding land and business ownership in Ireland, it has nothing intrinsically contradictory in it; of all the defenses available to one accused of being part of such a conspiracy character witnesses are not the ones most likely to be employed. The charges of hidden Fianna Fail interests in the area were so persistent that at its May 7, 1979, meeting the city council passed a motion calling on "any Councillors who may have a vested interest in Wood Quay and precincts to declare them." (Before the council's openness in the matter is allowed to cause admiration, it should be noted that passage of the motion was easy virtue, for the council was going out of office in a month, there would be no need for any of the councillors to comply before that time, and the resolution did not bind the next council.) Nothing would make the suspicion of Fianna Fail manipulation go away, and probably nothing ever will. The defenses against the charge are so repeatedly used as to be almost automatic: Sam Stephenson (who, as architect of the civic offices, will figure prominently in the Wood Quay story) said that the area was so run down that anyone who built in it, as he had, would be doing a public service; Pat Russell of the corporation's Development Department asked, what about all those people in the center city who are renting office space to the corporation which the corporation would no longer need when the new buildings were built—didn't they have a secret interest in preventing the offices from going up?

The most innocent explanation of the museum's actions (and curiously it does not seem to have been advanced by the museum itself) is that it was proceeding the way any archaeological authority in the British Isles would have proceeded in similar circumstances: when there is a conflict between archaeology and land development, agreements to surrender the land to the developers are always punctiliously observed—regardless of the value of the archaeological material. The reasoning behind this policy on the part of the archaeologists is that failure to surrender the land would cause developers to lose confidence in the archaeological community and make it more difficult for archaeologists in the future to negotiate limited access to archaeological sites prior to the commencement of work by the developers.

Peter Addyman, who is director of the Coppergate excavations in York, the site in England which is more like Wood Quay, although not so large, than any other in the British Isles, spoke of his practice; asked "What if it is clear that there are considerable riches still in the ground when the deadline [for handing over a site to builders] comes?" he replied:

> We accept that. In the Coppergate site at York we excavated one-tenth of the area to be destroyed. So nine-tenths of our site went. In fact, in the remaining nine-tenths was this remarkable helmet you may have read about, the Coppergate helmet, which has been insured recently for half a million pounds. It's a stupendous thing of the immediately pre-Viking period, a marvelous Northumbrian war helmet. The ornamentation on it was equal to anything in the Lindisfarne gospels, you know. . . . It was found by a bull-dozer. . . . The thing is absolutely stunning and does illustrate what is being lost not only in Dublin and York but all sorts of places.

On the basis of their public statements Lucas and Raftery can be assumed to have been of one mind with the British archaeologist. The strange thing that happened in Dublin was that the public was not so tolerant. In Dublin the public took over.

2. A CIVIC PLACE

WERE THERE no other sites on which the civic offices could have been built? There were plenty of other sites. The corporation, long practiced in answering the question, made out that really in the long run no place else in the whole city of Dublin was suitable, but in fact the corporation had considered other places and had given less than cogent reasons for rejecting them. And beyond those locations there were many derelict sites throughout the city which any Dubliner could point to and which were destined either for private development or for years more of dereliction. The north side of the city, so much in need of rescue and so rich in potential sites for the offices, would have been invigorated by the presence of a hub of official business.

The whole civic offices project is almost part of Dublin's ancient history. The initial proposal to build the offices was made back in 1901, when Ireland was still part of the British empire and James Joyce had not yet fled the country. At that time a proposal had been presented to the Improvements Committee of Dublin Corporation recommending the building of central offices for the city government on Lord Edward Street, which runs the two hundred yards or so from City Hall to Christ Church.

Forty years later another proposal was made, this one to widen Parliament Street (which intersects Lord Edward Street at the point proposed for the offices) and build the new civic offices on its west side. The area available for civic development would have been huge in comparison to the four acres finally settled on at Wood Quay; it would have stretched from Parliament Street to the west across the Wood Quay site all the way to Winetavern Street, but would have left the Winetavern end relatively free of building to insure an unobstructed view of Christ Church from the quays. In 1945 it was proposed that the Wood Quay part of the civic offices site be used for a public health institute, and in 1946 a recommendation was made by the city architect and planning officer that a competition be announced for designs for a combined health institute and municipal offices center. But none of the proposals of the 1940s bore fruit.

In December 1951 the office issue came to life again when the city council accepted a committee report that recommended the borrowing of £60,000 to erect corporation offices on Winetavern Street. After deliberations that ruled out several other sites (St. Anne's Park in Clontarf for one, which would have been a quite feasible location), the committee recommended in July 1954 deferring the erection of a civic center, but approved the erection of some offices on Winetavern Street to meet immediate needs. The estimated cost of these offices was £500,000.

In May 1955 the architectural firm of Jones and Kelly submitted sketch plans for the Winetavern office building which could in no way pass for an unpretentious substitute for the civic offices nor be reasonably referred to as an office block on Winetavern. The proposed building fronted the quays, stretched all the way from Winetavern to Fishamble, and presented a façade that seemed to be inspired by the Victor Emmanuel monument in Rome. It ran into strong objections.

In November 1960 An Coisde Cuspoiri Coiteann, the city council's general purposes committee, which had been considering the civic office proposals, recommended the acquisition of the whole square of land between Fishamble and Winetavern. The compulsory purchase order (eminent domain action) on the site was made in 1961 and confirmed after lengthy appeals in 1964. By 1967 most of the land had been acquired. No archaeological work had yet been started on Winetavern, but the brief prepared by the corporation to announce the invitation of construction bids did refer to the possibility of archaeological finds on the site.

So did several letters to editors of Dublin newspapers. Letters to editors do not ordinarily become part of the documentary history of events, but at least two of the letters that appeared in November 1968 were remarkable for their authors' grasp of the archaeological potential of the Wood Quay site and their prescience about the threats to it. Paddy Healy wrote a letter that appeared in the three morning papers between November 16 and 19, and Peter J. Walsh, now curator of the Guinness Museum, wrote one that appeared November 25 in the *Irish Times*. Together they came close to constituting the most researched compact statements on the Wood Quay site's potential that had been presented in any popular medium. This correspondence was published before any work had started on the Winetavern site and therefore before the Viking city wall was unearthed; the writers based their statements not on anything yet found but on what someone studying the site would conclude must be there.

The competition for development of the site ended with the selection of a design for four square tower blocks identical in plan and character, one of five, two of seven, and one of ten stories, proposed by the Green Property Company and designed by Stephenson, Gibney & Associates. Green Property was later the same year to gain itself a popular reputation for villainy by sending a gang of goons into a Georgian house on St. Stephen's Green East for the violent and bloody eviction of four young people who were occupying the house to prevent its destruction.

The planning permission was granted on Christmas Eve, December 24, 1970, a day when attention to public affairs was not at its peak. Nonetheless the granting of the permission did not go unnoticed, and before the time for filing objections ran out thirty-one separate parties had appealed the permission. The appeals were heard on May 6, 1971. Over a year later, on July 27, 1972, the minister for local government denied the appeals and affirmed the planning permission subject to some negligible conditions, most of them involving repositioning of the buildings and revision of the plans for the surrounding streets. While planning and financing efforts were under way Green Property withdrew from the scheme and the city decided that the project would go ahead without the developer but otherwise unchanged, that is, it would still be the Stephenson Gibney four-block collection.

Sam Stephenson and Arthur Gibney would soon go separate ways, setting up their own firms, and Stephenson Associates would become the architects for the civic offices. Although Sam Stephenson had been the architect involved in several major controversies between conservationists and developers—including the Green Property eviction mentioned above—he was on those occasions somewhat in the shadow of the developers, who took the brunt of the conservationists' attacks. But with the coming of the civic offices construction Stephenson came to center stage. He was a concrete presence, a Dublin personality, unlike many of the corporation and government figures involved in the controversy, who seemed more like abstract forces than real people.

Stephenson had attended the Jesuit-run Belvedere College that Joyce has immortalized and the Bolton Street College of Technology and had become professionally and socially prominent in Dublin. Newspapers reported his property dealings along with his architec-

ture, and he became associated in the popular mind with the powerful upper levels of Fianna Fail. He was a close friend of the future
taoiseach (prime minister), Charles Haughey; Stephenson's chauffer-
ing Haughey about after Haughey's resignation from the cabinet
when charged with gun-running in 1970 was a Fianna Fail vignette
that seemed to fascinate the public.

Stephenson looks like a dieting Peter Ustinov and has a person-
able manner. Friend and foe use the same expression to describe
him: Sam is a charmer. His quiet, reasonable explanations have an
air of the axiomatic; it seems an affront to logic not to be convinced
by them. The most disarming thing about them is that half of them
seem either extremely ingenuous or extremely disingenuous—it's
hard to know which. "Well, Father, all we can do now is pray," he
said to F. X. Martin when the latter came to warn him in 1978 that
his offices were going to be picketed by UCD and Bolton Street students over his role as architect of the civic offices. The quotation,
which has afforded Wood Quay activists some mirth, has to be
understood as having nothing of the sarcastic in it.

"If that had gone up," Stephenson said, contemplating a model
of a building that he had unsuccessfully proposed for a site near the
Grand Canal, "Dublin would have moved into the twenty-first century." That is his dream.

He has taken some steps toward realizing it. His early work like
the Electricity Supply Board buildings and some offices originally
proposed for the corner of St. Stephen's Green and Hume Street are
undistinguished—they look nine-tenths engineer and one-tenth architect—but some of his later buildings have flair. His Fitzwilliam
Lawn Tennis Club would be all right on an Ivy League campus. The
building he designed for Bord na Mona, the turf authority, is walled
with planes of reflecting glass, a now familiar but not bad-looking
style. It looks like a modest borrowing from downtown Stamford,
Connecticut. The only shortcoming, in fact, in most of Stephenson's
more recent buildings is that they reflect familiar trends. One would
not say that, however, of two of his creations, the Central Bank
building and Stephenson's own office on Bride Street, a converted
church which looks like the set of a James Bond movie.

The four office blocks which Stephenson designed for the civic
offices have been controversial not merely because of the project's
conflict with archaeology but also because of the buildings' appearance. The renderings of them published before construction began
and the finished look of the two now standing suggest function before all else. Lego blocks, a Dublin artist called them, and there is no
question that they are blockish. This quality is relieved a bit by bev-

eled edges and horizontal window patterns that seem to hover between the integral and the decorative. Stephenson said of them (re-
ferring to their redesign after James Tully, the minister for local
government, required that they be moved eastward on the site from
the position originally planned for them):

> As they got tighter together I wanted to make them much starker
> and simpler, prisms, really. A lot of classical buildings even have a
> lot of untidy things going on. We decided to tidy up and make it
> a definite form and shape. So the buildings will look like solid
> granite tubes, prisms, very deeply recessed slots. They will be
> quite solid elements against the tracery of the cathedral. . . . Very
> severe.

Even the buildings' defenders cannot ignore the way they crowd
Christ Church. Stephenson counters with a favorite argument the
charges that the buildings obstruct the view of the cathedral:

> One of the most impressive architectural experiences of my life
> has been the Cologne cathedral, an enormous building—the inte-
> rior of it just disappears—it goes up into the dark. It's a remark-
> able structure. It towers over you. You come up these little narrow
> streets in Cologne, and, bang, you see one side of the cathedral,
> one aspect of it. It is almost impossible to comprehend the cathe-
> dral in its totality from anywhere. That's a subjective view that a
> lot of people have that that's the way you should see the medieval
> cathedrals, not out in the broad open. So we in our earliest
> scheme placed all four buildings so that you got views through the
> complex of different aspects of the cathedral.

Cologne cathedral has the air of a found argument. More revealing about Stephenson's thinking is a statement of his quoted in the
January 13, 1985, *Sunday Tribune:*

> All great architecture seems to be put up by autocrats. De-
> mocracy has never produced great architecture. . . .
> You look at Albert Speer and the things that he and Hitler
> were up to—apart from the things that they'll be remembered for
> ultimately—they were really up to the most remarkable archi-
> tectural concept of the new Reich. They were going to build on
> a heroic scale that would have made the Roman Empire look
> pedantic. They were having a jolly time planning great urban
> complexes.
> And Speer was a very interesting architect. He was a most
> remarkable individual, very sensitive, a very good designer in the

classical sense, and clearly a man of great administrative ability. And the pity of it was their holocaust and the persecution of millions of people. But all the great cities of the world were put up by some sort of autocrat.

Back in 1973 when the financing of the construction work had just been approved, it took a bit of imagination to visualize the new Cologne cum Berlin. The land clearance that began in the summer of that year moved rapidly into the southeast corner of the site and cut extremely deeply; this was the period during which the giant JCB described by Paddy Healy penetrated the medieval habitation layers and during which a picture appeared in the *Irish Times* showing the bucket of a large excavator poised in the air silhouetted against the sky next to the tower of Christ Church as if it were really about to scoop up the cathedral.

Alarms about the danger to the archaeological material in general and the wall in particular led to an order in mid-November 1973 from James Tully, the minister for local government, stopping work on the buildings. The corporation reacted with distress; its public relations officer, Noel Carroll, cited the money already spent on the site and the irony that the finds on the site would never have been made if the corporation had not cleared it and asked the archaeologists in in the first place. The momentum behind the construction of the civic offices had just become tangible enough to make the prospect of relocating, issuing new CPOs (compulsory purchase orders), and arranging new financing nothing less than agonizing in the eyes of the corporation officials. In the eyes of the Local Government and Public Services Union (LGPSU) the prospect was outrageous. Harold O'Sullivan, general secretary of the union, which represented the workers who looked forward to working in the new buildings, spoke in vaguely threatening terms about exposing the use of space in some of the corporation's more makeshift offices, use which, it was suggested, would be shown to be illegal in terms of the Offices Premises Act.

In retrospect it is clear that not only would archaeology have been better off if the civic offices had not been built at Wood Quay, but so would the corporation and its employees. The LGPSU would not brook the delay that would result from the project's relocation to Waterford Street on the north side of the city (one of several proposals made after initial land clearance had started on the Wood Quay site), but, as things turned out, it would be October 1986 before the first office workers moved into the new buildings; if the offices had been moved to Waterford Street, they would almost certainly have been functioning sooner. The corporation argued the expense of relocating, since so much money had already been assigned to the work on the Wood Quay site (five million pounds, Noel Carroll was quoted as saying), but the delays caused by the controversy were going to send the costs off the graph; twenty-seven million pounds by June 1984, according to a statement of City Manager Frank Feely reported in the *Irish Times*.

Even worst-case thinking, however, would not have anticipated such delays. The corporation officials were realists: lots of things cause delays, but archaeology is not one of them.

3. NORMANS

N THE YEAR that followed the withdrawal of the archaeologists from the Winetavern digs in 1973 the whole archaeological site seemed to be in limbo. So did the projected civic offices. Then in May 1974 began serious archaeology on the Wood Quay site and serious threats to archaeology on the site. This contest lasted for two years until in July 1976 half time was called, and all players left the field. Half time lasted fifteen months.

It was during the active period between 1974 and 1976 that Wood Quay became a byword. The archaeologists made more extensive and important discoveries than ever before, the forces promoting the civic offices crowded and obstructed the archaeologists as never before, the elected representatives of the city and even of the state began to question what was going on, and the public began to mobilize to "save Wood Quay."

On July 25, 1973, the Winetavern Street excavations came to an end and the museum's archaeological team moved to the Christ Church Place excavation. The leveling of the Wood Quay site described earlier was completed in September 1973.

Early in November 1973 representatives of the corporation, the museum, and the architects met to plan the future of the site. Representing the museum were A. T. Lucas, Joseph Raftery, and Breandán Ó Ríordáin, who, as it happened, were to be the three successive directors of the museum during the Dublin excavations. Among the corporation representatives was Patrick J. Russell, whose title was assistant principal officer of the Development Department and who was to be the corporation official in charge of the building of the civic offices; as such he was on the leading edge of most conflicts between the corporation and the opponents of the civic offices. Sam Stephenson was present for his firm.

In his presentation Stephenson explained the plans for the offices and said that there was no reason why the construction work and the archaeology could not be carried on "in sympathy." Lucas stressed the unknown character of the site but suggested that the likelihood of finding medieval structures intact was remote and added that the museum was mainly interested in discovering and preserving artifacts. He was completely satisfied with the cooperation the corporation had given the museum, he said. Raftery echoed this feeling and called the corporation's proposals generous; the museum would support its views of the matter, he said, regardless of what was said by less well informed sources.

Raftery was very sensitive to ill-informed sources. His appointment three years later as head of the National Museum climaxed a career in archaeology that had gained him an international reputation and offices in several learned societies. Raftery was chairman of the National Monuments Advisory Council when the Wood Quay protests were at their most turbulent stage—the NMAC, an official body accurately described by its name, was to become an important participant in the archaeological controversy. Austere in appearance, he was sought out by reporters as the controversy developed and took advantage of interviews to decry the ignorance of the museum's critics: the leading protest groups were "half-wits" and the university archaeologists "part and parcel of the rabble." His interviews, however, were a great leap forward in public relations for the museum, for A. T. Lucas was able to say in 1981, several years after he retired as head of the museum, "I have never been quoted."

The solution Sam Stephenson proposed of leaving high-priority archaeological areas intact for two years and practically sheltering them under the building may have sounded good, but, as events proved, was totally unrealistic; even though plans were made to allow the city wall to run through the ground levels of the buildings to be built over it, with the rooms containing the wall turned into museum space, no archaeological work could be done on the large area required by the office buildings themselves or on adjacent work areas. The excavations for the foundations of the east block were to be among the most destructive operations on the site.

The Lucas remark about the museum's interest being in artifacts was an early statement of a philosophy that would later be affirmed by Raftery and repudiated by most of the archaeological effort's strongest advocates and by archaeologists themselves. Once the Wood Quay excavations had become advanced the great interest of the scholarly community was not in the artifacts but in the total evidence of the development of a culture, the signs of interests, health, domestic habits, commerce, imagination, and the patterning of town life.

On March 13, 1974, at another conference of the corporation, museum, and architects, the site was divided into three areas to be made available to the museum for varying periods of excavation. The map on the seventh page of the photo section shows the division of the site: area 1 was the northeast corner bordering part of Wood Quay and part of Fishamble Street as far up as the city wall; area 2 was south of area 1 and ran as far up Fishamble as the current land clearance permitted; area 3 bordered Winetavern Street. At this time it was agreed that area 1 would be available to the archaeologists for nine months (until December 1974), area 2 for two years (until March 1976), and area 3 for three years (until March 1977). A somewhat different timetable announced by the city manager at the city council meeting November 4, 1974, set the deadline for area 1 at March 31, 1975, and for area 2 at December 31, 1975.

The earliest reports of this three-area division made it seem that the museum would have nine months of unhindered work on area 1. Everything about the agreement except the shortness of the time seemed satisfactory, but at still another meeting May 13, 1974, of representatives of the museum, architects, and corporation it became clear that the museum did not have the elbow room that it first seemed to have, for the corporation required a good deal of area 1, fifteen feet in from the perimeter, to build a retaining wall.

The May 13 meeting was the most down-to-business so far because it coincided with the actual beginning of archaeological work in area 1, the beginning of the phase of the Dublin excavations that would come to be known as "Wood Quay" proper.

For these excavations the museum did not call Breandán Ó Ríordáin back from Christ Church Place but introduced a new figure to the Dublin archaeological scene. Patrick F. Wallace was only twenty-five when he was selected to head the Wood Quay campaign. Born in Limerick and educated, undergraduate and graduate, at University College Galway, he went to work for the museum on leaving school and was put in charge of an important medieval dig, the Oyster Lane excavations in Wexford. In April 1974 he was called up to the museum and told his new assignment. "It was a four-acre site," Wallace said. "I was numb."

The reaction was understandable. Wallace, however, was constitutionally as well as professionally equipped to face the four acres. He is of medium height and build, and seems to be put together in the solid way farmers and seamen are. Later in the course of the Wood Quay drama he was called a peasant; the epithet pleased him and he enjoyed repeating it, not because it was a complimentary Joan of Arc allusion, but because it was an image he felt comfortable with. Confrontations with the construction crews on the site he was always ready to take in stride, he said. "I'm an outdoor digger and I can talk to engineers and I can fight with engineers. . . . A digger or a bulldozer is no problem—you can stop it, chat up the guy . . ." When he talks about work on the site, he is precise, fluent, and graphic—a perfect television interviewee—but from time to time a droll, sarcastic, or earthy remark slips out of the corner of his mouth as if a second self were talking, and he follows it with a smile that looks more intensely amused than most people's laughter. Looking back over his work at Wood Quay shortly after it ended, Wallace capsulized his philosophy of the site: "Finds seem to be the thing. They are not. What you have here is a total town—streets, houses, the layout, the original city townscape, town planning. That's what's important. Environment, not . . . another twopenny game piece. There's millions of those."

About the area that Wallace and his crew started excavating in May one thing was known in advance: it was all landfill built up to move the shoreline out into a deeper part of the Liffey to allow docking for larger ships. This in itself did not tell much about what would be found there; it might be nothing but mud and gravel.

Starting on this part of the site the archaeologists were working backward through the centuries, for the earlier settlements, those of the Vikings, lay uphill to the south near Christ Church. That was the area that the Winetavern digs had been sampling. Naturally the first landfill occurred up there and was the work of the Vikings. The fill down near the river was the last and was the work of the Normans. Working backward was no liability for the archaeologists; at least it would not have been if they could have assumed that the earliest area would still be waiting when the excavations got that far.

The digs had not been under way long when the first discoveries were made. The most dramatic was a wooden structure paralleling the river. It was recognized as a seawall or quay built at the limit of one of the advances into the river. Its elaborateness and engineering struck the archaeologists at once. Pat Wallace described it in a May 1979 article in the magazine *An Cosantoir:* "a stout wooden framework or revetment . . . built of oak uprights behind which were placed horizontal planks set on edge and held in place by the pressure of backfill and town refuse which were heaped behind. The uprights were mortised into footbeams [baseplates] and were braced on the waterside by raking-struts which were mortised and tenoned into soleplates fixed at right angles to the footbeams." This most advanced of all the structures used so far in the extension of the land was dated by the archaeologists about the year 1210. Behind this re-

vetment to the south were found six lines of timbers of similar nature which might have been part of earlier attempts to reclaim the
land or which might have been property boundaries.

The landfill behind the revetment was town refuse mixed with
mud and gravel from the river. On top of this were placed layers
of wickerwork, then cobbled pathways, and eventually large footbeams. Close by the revetment were found remains of what was apparently a dockside warehouse erected there to house cargo.

The dating of the major revetment indicates the energy with
which the Normans extended the town; all of this fill and construction work had taken place within forty years of the Norman arrival
in Dublin and had advanced the shoreline more than twice as far as
the Vikings had advanced it in their three centuries of residence. Reporting the discovery of the revetment, some news stories speculated that what the archaeologists had found was the original "Wood
Quay." Historians did not rally to that bit of onomastics, which
would certainly have romanticized the revetment if true. Pat Wallace voiced the general view when he attributed the name Wood
Quay to the use of that point on the shore in the middle ages for the
unloading of wood or possibly woad used in dyeing.

In a conversation three months after all work on the site ended
in 1981, Pat Wallace commented on the importance of what the archaeologists had learned from all the carpentry on the site:

> We do not have the timbered buildings that they have all over
> England, so our knowledge of Irish carpentry is very small. Now
> that we have the stuff from this Dublin excavation we can say a
> good deal about the carpentry of Ireland . . . In the beginning Dub-
> lin carpentry was not of a very high standard, but in its later
> stages it was. My reason for that is that Dublin became Hiber-
> nicized in the middle of the eleventh century. We know that there
> was already a high standard of carpentry in native contexts in
> Ireland and that crept into Dublin. When the Normans came,
> they, who had achieved very good carpentry in England, did not
> introduce their technique but continued to use the Irish-Norse
> carpenters.

The newly found revetment offered a good lesson in Norman
carpentry. The tools most used in building it were apparently chis-
els, spoon bits, and adzes; there was little sign of sawed wood. Joining was by doweling and mortising rather than by nails, and the
structure seems to have been prefabricated. One of the problems the
builders faced was contending with the pressure put on the wall by

the landfill behind it; in time they added additional uprights between the main uprights of the revetment.

The archaeologists discovered that shortly after the building of the revetment a farther advance had been made into the river, this time by construction of a second revetment fifty feet beyond the first. This revetment was made of old ships' timbers, some of them still joined. When the second revetment collapsed, a third, still farther out into the river, was built. This strong and cleverly designed extension was not to be the last, for it was itself superseded by a stone quay built some time in the early 1300s. This stone wall was the last of the landfill extensions; it stood about forty feet from the present walled edge of the river.

At right angles to the successive revetments ran drains made of reused ships' timbers and apparently connected with wooden tanks on the higher levels constituting at least in the case of one tank, if the archaeologists' interpretation of their function is correct, a sophisticated waste-disposal system: at high tide a sluice gate would be opened, admitting the river water into the tanks, and at low tide the gate would be opened again, allowing the water along with waste disposed of in the tanks to be carried out into the river. The covered drain tops apparently served as footpaths; two of the drains were redone in the later middle ages in stone and continued in use down to the eighteenth century.

The numerous parts of thirteenth-century ships that were found became more interesting when dendrochronologist Michael Baillie confirmed that the timbers were of Irish origin, for historical records suggested that shipbuilding and exporting were Dublin industries during the middle ages. These ships or ship parts would form the only extant trace of the industry.

The artifacts found on the waterfront site were multitudinous; in the first six months of the dig about fifty thousand were turned up. The pottery fragments indicated trade routes. From England the majority of pottery pieces were of Bristol origin, especially "Ham Green" ware, an origin which is not surprising in view of the close ties created between Bristol and Ireland by Henry II's grant of Dublin to his "men of Bristol."

Enough clothing of woolen and linen fabrics was found to give some indication of dress styles. Jewelry, ornaments, boots, shoes, and knife sheaths abounded as they had on the Viking sites. There were padlocks, keys, scales, lamps, knives, bowls, hammers, axes, drill bits, fishhooks, horseshoes, spurs, grindstones, dice, game pieces, coins, pilgrims' flasks, and what seemed to be parts of religious reliquaries. Meat bones, shells, and other indications of diet turned up, and as on the Winetavern site there was a piggy bank—but this one had a thirteenth-century coin inside it. And this was the part of the Wood Quay site that was universally regarded as being of least importance.

A harvest of medieval material at least equal in size to the archaeologists' discoveries was, however, being made by the earthmovers. Construction on the retaining wall was proceeding so close to the digs that the archaeologists could often reach out and touch the earthmoving equipment. Day after day the trucks left the site loaded with the same kind of material that the archaeologists were turning up.

Among conservationists and then among readers of the Irish newspapers a realization began to dawn of just how much of medieval Dublin had been trucked away. Not much attention had been paid to the medieval material lost during the site leveling, but now the papers showed pictures of trucks being filled from the excavations for the retaining wall.

So much of medieval Dublin had been transferred to the Ringsend dump that people began to comb the dump putting together their own medieval collections. It was in May 1975, about one year after the archaeological and construction work on Wood Quay began, that press reports described the discovery of the medieval material at the dump. John O'Loughlin Kennedy, the executive officer of An Taisce, described his own finds at the dump and added that they had to be viewed in the light of the common archaeological axiom about the importance of context to finds; the treasures that turned up at the dump would be of little instructive value once removed from their original site. (In 1982 the *Evening Press* told the story of Pat O'Mara, a Dublin workingman, who found enough artifacts on a roadside near Phoenix Park en route to the site of a later dumping of Wood Quay material to set up a Wood Quay display in the Ballyfermot Public Library; the surplus of his finds he gave to the National Museum and the Dublin Civic Museum.)

For a month before he spoke out about his finds at the dump, Kennedy, who is thought by many conservationists to have given An Taisce the most vigorous leadership in its history, had been hounding the corporation for allowing the construction work to damage archaeological material. On April 7, 1975, An Taisce issued a statement at a press conference near Wood Quay. The statement began:

> An Taisce today calls on whoever is in charge of the Winetavern
> Street Site where Dublin Corporation proposes to build its new

offices to put an end to the vandalism which is occurring there. Medieval timber structures are being smashed by mechanical diggers and bulldozers. Over the week-end it came to the notice of An Taisce that, despite assurances to the contrary, substantial medieval structures have been damaged and partially swept away without archaeological investigation. . . . The bulldozers came within two feet of one most valuable find, the remains of a medieval boat, before it was hurriedly surveyed and removed in pieces.

The statement ended with an invitation to the press to come on the site and photograph the evidence; when a Radio Telefís Éireann television crew and a number of journalists took up the invitation and accompanied Kennedy onto the site, Noel Carroll, the public relations officer of the corporation, arrived and charged Kennedy with "a serious breach of ethics" for coming on the site without permission. An angry exchange ensued, which the reporters were delighted to record.

In press reports of discussions in the city council meeting of May 5, 1975, City Manager Matthew Macken was quoted as saying that the claims of removal of archaeological material by construction company excavators may have been accurate. "If it happened, it had happened."

Realizing that archaeological work on the site did not finally come to an end until 1981, one will expect to learn that the archaeologists were given further extensions of their deadlines. So they were, right down to the end, often very short ones—three months, two months, six weeks.

Back on March 12, 1974, the day before the corporation, museum, and architects met to make the three-area division of the site, a meeting of another sort had been held. This one was a public gathering organized by the Living City Group and held at the Mansion House, the building which serves as residence of the lord mayor and as a public meeting and exhibition hall. The Living City Group is a small, energetic organization devoted to studying worldwide planning initiatives and alerting Dubliners to long-range threats to their neighborhoods from planning proposals currently under consideration; its newspaper, *City Views*, which suspended publication at the end of 1981 because of the expiration of a grant on which it depended, would constitute, if back issues were collected, a handbook on Dublin development. The gathering was the first large, public Wood Quay protest meeting and was the harbinger of the coming public involvement in the fate of the archaeological site.

Deirdre Kelly, the moving force behind the meeting, had been

Deirdre McMahon when, still in school, she gained renown as an organizer of the efforts to save Dublin's Georgian houses. In 1970 she had been a leader of the protesters who occupied a Georgian house on St. Stephen's Green to save it from demolition (which they succeeded in doing for half a year until violently thrown out of the building by goons hired by the developer). Married now to Aidan Kelly, an architect, she has continued to be prominent on the conservation scene partly because of her role as head of the Living City Group, her editing of *City Views*, and her authorship of *Hands Off Dublin* (1976), a book on the city's endangered neighborhoods, but also because she became recognized as a kind of personal archive of urban environmental information and of Dublin planning realities.

As in her student days she talks fast, smiles fast, and has a dry wit which comes and goes fast. She has frazzled, cute good looks and a charm that is relaxed almost to the point of being distracted. One would get a pretty typical impression of her watching her meet a couple of writers at a favorite pub in Rathmines, get cheery greetings down the length of the bar, and settle down to talk of the excessive work load of the city's building inspectors in such an authoritative way that ears from adjoining tables telescope in to the conversation.

For the Mansion House meeting she had assembled a group of specialists, some of whom were to become prominent in the developing effort to save the archaeological site. George Eogan, professor of archaeology at UCD recognized for his work on the prehistoric remains at Knowth in the Boyne Valley, observed that Viking studies everywhere were waiting on the Dublin excavations, and that even the Norman finds on the site were taking on an importance no one had anticipated. Richard Haworth, an archaeologist with the state-sponsored planning and research body An Foras Forbartha and subsequently geography librarian at Trinity College and a conspicuous Wood Quay activist, spoke of financing the archaeological work through contributions by the developers, a sanguine-sounding proposal but in fact a realistic one, as the funding by several Irish industries of archaeological work on their property would shortly prove. Thomas Delaney, a Belfast archaeologist whose early death in 1979 was to sadden his colleagues in the Wood Quay cause, spoke of the experiences of other European cities with comparable archaeological treasures. Nuala Burke, a geographer specializing in Dublin's medieval history, spoke of the expectations for the Wood Quay site created by a close study of the documentary history of the area. Archaeologist and author Peter Harbison spoke of the need for a crisis-motivated expansion of the archaeological work force.

In August 1974 An Taisce called for a greatly expanded archaeological work force, and in September and November jointly signed letters from well-known Irish historians and archaeologists supported An Taisce's call and pleaded for the safety of the archaeological site.

The corporation continued to reassure, but its reassurances became less reassuring as scrutiny of official plans for the site increased. The city council was brought into the business of the civic offices toward the end of 1974; supportive of the corporation's plans at first, it eventually became a major source of criticism of the archaeological site's treatment. Its meetings became the most important forum of argument over Wood Quay.

4. SCRUTINY

T HE CITY COUNCIL'S attention to Wood Quay will seem natural. It *was* natural, to be sure, and it probably would have produced a clear policy about the archaeological site if the council were not so enervated and fettered. Although the council is Dublin's elected governing body and, as such, probably the second most important elected body in the nation after the Dáil, it acts in combination with a city manager and an appointed bureaucracy who have such resources and legal power that they can overcome almost any initiative on the part of the councillors. In most of their official actions the bureaucracy and the council are in accord, but when the bureaucracy is challenged by the council, the real locus of power is the city manager.

The council's traditional tolerance of its negative balance of power broke down in the course of the Wood Quay controversy. Confrontations over the archaeological site reached an exceptional intransigence and illustrated how much power the city manager could wield when he had to and how effectively he could stifle council action.

At the end of 1974, however, as Pat Wallace's excavators worked on the Norman material by the river and Breandán Ó Ríordáin excavated Christ Church Place, there were no confrontations in the city council, because none of the councillors knew enough about what was going on on the sites even to raise pertinent questions. Alderman Carmencita Hederman, who would become the lord mayor of Dublin in 1987, quite rightly takes credit for being one of the first councillors to pay attention to Wood Quay:

> I was in on it very, very early. What I found that was extremely
> upsetting about it was that the only other people on the city coun-
> cil who had any interest in it were Kevin Byrne and Sean Dublin
> Bay Loftus. I remember bringing it up with them one day before

a meeting and I said to them, "You've heard about this Wood Quay thing, haven't you?" This was before I knew whether there was anything genuinely in it or not, and they were very interested.
I brought it up that night at a meeting, and Kevin and Sean were the only ones who supported me. In fact I was sort of cross when Kevin tried to take it over from me, but I didn't really mind. For a long time—I don't know if it was a year or eighteen months— none of the archaeologists in Dublin was prepared to come out and support us. So the situation I was in—Kevin Byrne didn't mind because he was a different kind of person—was that here I was getting up in the city council saying all kinds of things and finding that there was nobody whom we respected in the archaeo-logical field who'd come out and say it. They were all prepared to ring me up and say, "You've got to do something about it," but none of them would come out in the open. And I can remember coming back from a meeting after it had been going on for eigh-teen months and saying to my husband, "I'm just browned off at this. Here are Sean and Kevin and I, lone voices, and other mem-bers of the city council are saying, 'Who's she? What does she know?'" And I am the first to admit that I am no experienced ar-chaeologist. Kevin Byrne was a different kind of person. He *was* prepared to say, "I'm an experienced archaeologist." Kevin was an expert on everything. (Interview, June 29, 1981)

The wildly original and politically manipulative Byrne was in-deed a different kind of person from the petite and refined surgeon's wife, but the Hederman-Byrne team worked well together. They drew the attention of the city council to the Wood Quay issue two years before the leading Wood Quay activist organization was founded and before Wood Quay became a popular cause. Byrne did, as a matter of fact, have a certain right to claim archaeological exper-tise, for he had studied archaeology under Ruaidhrí de Valera at Uni-versity College Dublin. What Byrne said in a memo to the city coun-cil on October 7, 1974, the day the council voted to approve the initial construction work on the Wood Quay site, would not have been noteworthy if said five years later but was remarkably far-seeing at the time it was written. The council, Byrne cautioned, had no information from the site archaeologist on the implications of the planned construction work, and museum statements on the matter were not adequate. He compared Wood Quay to urban ar-chaeology elsewhere and suggested that the danger of destroying Dublin's archaeological riches were greater than anyone acknowl-edged. At the meeting Byrne tried to defer commencement of construction work on the perimeter of the site, the retaining-wall work, by amending a motion, but his amendment was voted down.

By the spring of 1975 the council was raising questions and directing them not merely at the corporation's Development Department but at the museum, specifically at Lucas and Raftery. These two officials appeared before the city council meeting in committee on April 8, 1975. The *Irish Times* reported that Raftery expressed himself as satisfied that he had taken a broadly based survey of the site; he also said when asked about timbers taken from the site that he thought it likely that they were from eighteenth-century buildings. (About two weeks later, in an interview with Michael Viney of the *Irish Times*, Raftery said, "but when I gave that opinion to the Council I did say, 'I could be wrong.' That was not reported.") When the subject of additional time for the excavation was raised, the same article reported, Lucas and Raftery indicated that they were not likely to need it. (The extension of time for area 1 that the museum was working under at the time of the meeting with the council was a six-week one due to run out in mid-May.) Not likely to need more time? This was two years after Lucas had said that the museum was in the concluding stages of its final investigations; the suggestion that work was almost finished was as implausible at this stage as it had been in 1973, for the main Viking area of the site— the most important part—had scarcely been sampled. Carmencita Hederman asked two questions at this meeting which seem to have gone unanswered: How was it possible to bring the Wood Quay excavations to an end so quickly when it had taken years to study the little High Street site? And why should archaeologists outside the museum who had no vested interest in the site express opinions so at odds with the official museum statements?

April and May were to be an embarrassing time for the museum. On April 12, 1975, four days after the council meeting just spoken of, the *Irish Times* ran an editorial entitled "The Experts," which said in part:

> The Corporation and the city councillors have had no option but to accept and approve the archaeological policy of the director of the National Museum, Dr. Anthony Lucas, and his Keeper of Irish Antiquities, Dr. Joseph Raftery (who, unlike Dr. Lucas, is an archaeologist by discipline). It is these two men who have decided how much of the medieval area of the Wood Quay site should be explored and fully excavated, and how much time is needed for the job. . . . If office bestows authority, who is to argue with two such eminent men? If they settled for a part rather than a whole,

for a chapter rather than a book, who is to establish that this is the case—or even say that it is wrong? . . . It is at least strongly arguable by now that the scale of the Wood Quay potential for Dublin's archaeology has simply overwhelmed the capacities of the National Museum and that compromise has been obscured by a calculated aloofness and some bureaucratic discipline . . .

The *Times's* question, "who is to argue with two such eminent men?" did not go without an answer. The answer was: an independent archaeological body. Such a body had, in fact, been proposed a year before at the March 12, 1974, Mansion House meeting and later, in November 1974, when forty-one prominent Irish academics cosigned a letter to the Dublin papers about the excavations. On March 21, 1975, the Association of Young Irish Archaeologists raised the idea. But during April and May 1975 the suggestion came from all sides.

On April 15, 1975, a letter to the *Irish Times* suggested that the Wood Quay site was "an archaeological area of the highest significance, not just for Ireland, but for the whole study of medieval urban history in Europe" and found it "imperative that an independent commission of experts be established without delay to assess the whole position." The signers were George Eogan and Kevin B. Nowlan, who have been mentioned earlier, and Francis John Byrne and Donal McCartney, members of the history faculty at UCD. It was a heavyweight group. Byrne, one of the editors of Oxford's multivolume *A New History of Ireland*, is one of Ireland's best historians. On April 16 Senator Mary Robinson, speaking about the National Museum in the senate (primarily to ask that the reports of the museum's board of visitors, now four years old and never published, be made available to the Oireachtas), adverted to the Wood Quay situation and called for an overall scrutiny body to supervise the excavation and reporting of future archaeological digs. Gus Martin, another senator, raised the question of the appointment of a city archaeologist distinct from the museum. (Toward the end of 1975 that proposal was taken up in several quarters, and for a while it seemed that Dublin would get a city archaeologist, but that idea was finally abandoned.)

On April 18, 1975, John Jackson, the chairman of An Taisce, wrote to the lord mayor:

The advice of the National Museum can no longer be relied upon to achieve the objectives of the Corporation [described by the lord mayor in an April 9 letter to An Taisce as "to ensure that every feature of our past, on the Wood Quay site, is suitably excavated, examined and recorded"]. . . . An Taisce would respectfully suggest that the Corporation seek advice from a wider commission . . .

Around the end of April 1975 Professor R. Dudley Edwards of University College Dublin released to the press an inside report on the Wood Quay excavations, the first bit of news leaking in the controversy. The report, written by an unnamed archaeological assistant on the site, stressed the disparity between the amount of archaeological material to be excavated and the shortness of time allowed. Proper archaeological removal was out of the question when "the workers on the excavations were only hours ahead of the mechanical digger." The criticism was not directed, the writer said, at Pat Wallace or the excavation technique, but at the manner in which the National Museum supervised the excavations. "It is even more unfortunate that this feeling of dissatisfaction is shared by the staff working on the site." The report called on the museum to collaborate with medieval historians.

On April 25, 1975, the Geographical Society of Ireland and the Archaeological Society of UCD called for an independent commission to investigate the excavations. Even City Manager Macken, according to press reports May 6, 1975, seemed to favor the idea of a new archaeological authority. On May 13 the Irish Committee of Historical Sciences, the body representing both the republic and Northern Ireland in the International Historical Congress, wrote to the taoiseach asking for the establishment of a broadly based committee of historians, geographers, and planners to advise on Wood Quay and comparable medieval sites as yet unexcavated.

If the museum officials had begun to feel that April was the cruelest month, they probably treasured, if they had occasion to see it, Lord Mayor James O'Keeffe's April 22 reply to the An Taisce request for an independent body. The lord mayor admonished the conservationists that it would violate the proper relations between government authorities if the corporation sought advice on archaeology from some source other than the National Museum. The museum officials were also consistently defended by one archaeologist, Etienne Rynne, a faculty member at University College Galway. In an April 16, 1975, letter to the *Irish Times* he wrote:

> It is a well-known dictum among all archaeologists that the most competent to judge any excavation is generally the archaeologist excavating the site. There are exceptional cases, of course, but only when the excavating archaeologist is not as competent as the

critic. For anyone, above all a non-archaeologist, to suggest that all the National Museum is doing now "is digging up interesting material and saying it is satisfied" [as historical geographer Nuala Burke had said] is surely libellous. Might I suggest that she be . . . handed a scalpel and asked to remove an appendix, or given all facilities and asked to split the atom.

Etienne Rynne is A. T. Lucas's son-in-law. His *ad hominem* attack missed the mark, for the museum's scientific competence was not being questioned but its policy, and its critics were not exceeding their competence; one does not need a driver's license to recognize reckless driving.

The city council's increased involvement in the archaeological effort led to a second meeting in April with Lucas and Raftery. The first, on April 8, 1975, had resulted in an acceptance by the majority of the councillors of the museum officials' optimistic view of the archaeological work. Reports of the councillors' second meeting with the two officials on April 25, 1975, however, pictured the councillors as less satisfied and more probing. Councillor Ruairi Quinn, Michael Viney reported in the *Irish Times*, asked Raftery why he and Lucas were not more prepared to take part in public debate. "Because we're not in the dock," Raftery replied.

Debate, in any event, is precisely what the council was prepared to offer the museum officials. Alderman Alexis Fitzgerald presented a motion seconded by Carmencita Hederman that the council arrange a debate between the museum and An Taisce, at which the council would be observers. A formal recommendation of this debate—or "meeting"—was passed at the council's next regular meeting. On May 9, 1975, the principal officer of the Development Department, G. Hegarty, wrote to Lucas asking if he was prepared to comply with the council's recommendation. Lucas's reply, May 16, concluded:

> While, therefore, we deeply appreciate the good will of the Lord Mayor and the Council in recommending that a meeting be held between representatives of An Taisce and the Museum, we hope they will understand why we cannot see that any useful purpose would be served by participating in a meeting where the Museum staff would be subjected to an interrogation on their scientific work. We are, of course, always willing to explain to interested parties the procedure for archaeological excavation and the nature and extent of our work on particular sites. We have already explained this to members of the City Council and to other groups and in our view this should be sufficient to satisfy all but the most unreasonable.

The archaeological work went on. It became daily clearer how the development-minded Normans had envisioned their Dublin. Their rapid expansion of the waterfront out into the river deepened the quay area and allowed the docking and unloading of larger and larger ships. The first half-year of work on the area by the river had suggested a growing volume of trade and also suggested that if the excavations could proceed uphill to the south, a picture of the whole commercial area of early Dublin would be revealed.

Part of the interest in the discoveries at this point derived from the long-recognized differences between the Vikings and the Normans. The Vikings had been the adventurers and the Normans the capitalists. It was easy enough to speculate about what effect their respective characters must have had on the way they built up the trade and commerce of the city: was it comparable to the successive movements of frontier explorers and developers across the North American continent? And for the same reasons—that the latter were rationalizers and pragmatists? The farther the riverside excavations went, the less it was necessary to speculate, for the Norman plan continued to reveal itself and, as it did so, to strengthen the impression that the Normans, with their rapid port development schemes, were indeed the capitalists moving in on a relatively spontaneous and commercially innocent population. It is a good exhibit to put alongside the rationalized language used by Henry II when he authorized his Norman knights to serve under Dermot MacMurrough.

Artifacts continued not merely to turn up but almost to swamp the excavators. By the spring of 1975, eight months after work had started on the site by the river, the number of finds was put at eighty thousand.

In May 1975 the corporation announced the withdrawal of the construction company's mechanical excavators. That sounded like a boon to the archaeologists, but what it came down to was apparently nothing more than a ban on the mechanical excavators cutting into the archaeologists' territory, for the construction work on the retaining wall continued. At one point the construction hammers contacted and chipped into some stones thought by several authorities to be Fyan's Tower, part of that stretch of the old city wall that ran along the river. Most of the stones were left in place and cemented over in the course of the construction work.

About half a year before he ended his excavations at Christ Church Place in January 1976, Breandán Ó Ríordáin brought some of his workers down to join the Wood Quay excavators; Ó Ríordáin's band went to work on area 2 along Fishamble Street in late summer 1975. They were working at the top of the cliff created by the initial

land clearance two years before. It was in this area that the excavators were going to unearth the medieval habitations which
would constitute the most extensive "neighborhood" turned up
anywhere in medieval Dublin: ten homes with property lines and
floor plans that had remained constant through thirteen layers of
successive building and rebuilding. The plots were trapezoidal and
followed the line of present-day Fishamble Street, confirming more
convincingly than any other discovery the medieval origin of the
street patterns in that part of Dublin. The full extent of these habitations, however, was not discovered during the 1975–1976 digging;
it would be several more years before the archaeologists worked
through this area.

Breandán Ó Ríordáin's team, starting work at the south end of
the site and therefore south of the old city wall, made a discovery
which rivaled the city wall in importance. Parallel to the wall were
massive mudbanks constructed to serve as the earliest riverfront
barrier, obviously built by the Vikings and obviously older than the
city wall. They stood farther back into the Viking town and marked
off the town's earlier limits. They indicated where habitations pre-
ceding their construction would have lain; if they could be accurately dated, they would provide a control on the dating of any construction found behind them. They raised many questions: how far
did their east-west line extend? Was this where the longphort had
been built or were there other river barriers even farther south? Why
were the banks built—defense, flood control, some other reason?
How were they built? Ó Ríordáin had started working on them late
in 1975 but had not completed excavation when work on the site
was interrupted in 1976. The historical importance of the banks was
evident; their political significance in the future progress of work on
the Wood Quay site was going to be monumental.

In May 1976 reports began to appear that the civic offices were
in financial trouble. Although the city manager, when asked about
the state of the offices project, assured the city council that "No delays are envisaged regarding progressing the construction," the progressing seemed confined to paper work. Not only was no building
under way on the site, but it was not even known where on the site
the first buildings would be built; that surprise was being saved
for 1977.

Obviously the builders' absence from the site was a golden
opportunity for the archaeologists. The corporation enhanced the
opportunity with an offer of another extension of time. The opportunity more than slipped through the museum's fingers; it was
dropped with a thud. On July 7, 1976, the day before his resignation

as director of the museum was announced in the papers, Lucas wrote to the corporation declining to take advantage of the additional time offered and announcing that the museum was withdrawing from the site.

That was all. That anxiety which is bred by a tender sense of public relations was kept as far from the museum as the crowds of demonstrators who periodically collect behind wooden barriers in Kildare Street in front of the museum's next-door neighbor, the Oireachtas. There was no word as to what was going to become of the mudbanks and of the first signs of the habitations on Fishamble. Luxuriant weeds quickly covered the Wood Quay site. Archaeological soil is very rich, Pat Wallace said.

5. FRIENDS

N 1976 the theme of the annual Dublin Arts Festival was "Medieval Dublin." A by-product of the festival was the formation of a group which named itself the Friends of Medieval Dublin. When it first met on April 8, 1976, it was composed of a handful of well-known historians, geographers, and archaeologists from the two universities and a few other people who shared their interests.

No name stood out on the roster of the Friends more than that of its chairman, the Rev. Francis X. Martin, O.S.A., at the time head of the Department of Medieval History at University College Dublin. In the public mind he quickly *became* the Friends of Medieval Dublin and in the same public mind he emerged as the energizer and strategist of the movement to save Wood Quay.

Born in 1922, the son of a prominent Dublin doctor, Jesuit educated at Belvedere College, Martin joined the Augustinian friars (Luther's order, he notes), and was ordained a priest after studying for his first degrees in Rome and Dublin. He got his Ph.D. in history from Cambridge and has taught medieval history at UCD since 1962. His books on medieval and Irish history have been published in the British Isles and America, and he is currently an editor of the multi-volume Oxford history of Ireland, *A New History of Ireland.*

He works almost through the night and describes his summer trips to Italy as working vacations. "I'm going to take a vacation," he said, "I've set aside two weeks four summers from now." An enjoyable five-minute conversation seems to pick him up the way a night in a pub would another man.

Before the events at Wood Quay F. X. Martin had not been a public agitator. From his reputation as a scholar and from the orthodox, regular, and, in fact, clerical character of his immediate family one would not easily foresee the role he would end up playing in the Wood Quay drama. His three brothers became priests; one had been

a secretary to Dublin's powerful former archbishop, Charles Mc-
Quaid, and the other two professors of biblical studies and philoso-
phy. On his mother's side of the family, the Fitzmaurices of Lixnaw,
North Kerry, every generation back to the eighteenth century had
produced priests; there were even two twentieth-century bishops (of
Erie, Pennsylvania, and Wilmington, Delaware) in the family tree.

On his father's side, however, the family tradition was more
turbulent and more likely to produce a radical. He describes his
great-grandfather, Malachy Martin, who died in 1861, as a never-
captured fugitive from British justice in Ireland for eleven years. His
grandfather, James, who died in 1911, was publicly a schoolteacher
at Murroe, County Limerick, and secretly a central figure in the
Irish Republican Brotherhood group in East Limerick. His father,
Conor, was a medical officer to the Irish Volunteers in North Kerry
during the war of independence, 1919–1923.

No one in his family is better known in the United States than
his brother Malachi, the provocative author of *The Decline and Fall
of the Roman Church, The Encounter, Hostages to the Devil,* and
other books. Malachi Martin's controversial and alarmist analyses of
modern society draw on comparative religion, realpolitik, a disen-
chanted insider's savvy of the ecclesiastical, a private spirituality
that seems schooled in the old ascetics and mystics, and an apoca-
lyptic sense of his times.

F. X. Martin's scholarly work is primarily on medieval subjects,
but several of his writings deal with the Irish rebellion and the origins of modern Ireland. These would win him a certain favor with
those Irish readers who want history to lie down with nationalism,
but the favor might be jeopardized by a reading of Martin on the
Normans in Ireland.

What he has to say on the Normans is probably his most revisionist contribution to Irish history: he denies that there ever was
a Norman conquest or invasion of Ireland. Even though he had used
the term invasion in some of his writing in the 1960s, be began
in the next decade to question the standard readings of Irish historians on the period and to speak instead of the Norman "arrival" in
Ireland.

There is an interest which attaches to this interpretation of Professor Martin's which goes beyond the scholarly; it even goes beyond
the political significance (the beginning of English domination of
Ireland) that nationalists and the Irish in general attach to the coming of the Normans. The interest is that the redemption of the Normans' reputation is being undertaken by a Norman. It is not so important that F. X. Martin is in fact of Norman stock on both the

Martin and Fitzmaurice sides of his family, although that is a curiosity, as it is that he thinks and acts like a Norman in the midst of Gaels. He is rational, original, critical, organized, sophisticated about the use of power, focused in his energy, and tireless.

He thinks that the unfortunate thing about the spread of Norman power over Ireland is not that it happened but that it was not fully successful—it would have "made" Ireland. Dermot MacMurrough was not only not a villain for inviting the Normans; he was the most promising leader in the country. Henry II did not aspire to control Ireland, but merely sought to be assured that his Norman subjects in Ireland remained loyal to him. Dermot MacMurrough, if he had lived, would have been the most effective Irish leader to deal with Henry. St. Lawrence O'Toole, bishop of Dublin and MacMurrough's brother-in-law, would not have been as effective a leader of the Irish, being insufficiently Machiavellian.

In retrospect F. X. Martin's part in the Wood Quay agitation looks like a belated Norman victory, if victory is the right word, but, as in the days of Strongbow and MacMurrough, it was only a partial victory. Both the twelfth- and the twentieth-century Gaels look, in the eyes of the Norman, passionate, undirected, and self-defeating. The Norman in their midst has more power than they, but not quite enough to save the whole scene.

In 1976 neither the Friends nor their chairman had "gone public" about Wood Quay to any great extent. The Wood Quay excavations had been brought to a stop three months after the Friends were founded, and it took a little time to evolve the right strategy for dealing with a void. Also, the Friends, being heavily academic, gravitated toward educational approaches to the problem of saving medieval Dublin and, to some extent, toward correspondence with elected and appointed officials.

All that would be changed utterly in a year and a half. When the Friends did go public, F. X. Martin became the embodiment of the Wood Quay cause, evoking passionate loyalty and passionate hostility: the little boy standing in the street at a public demonstration with a placard reading "Francis Saviour Martin for Pope" and Charlie Haughey, later taoiseach, opining that "that (expletive deleted) mendicant friar ought to be thrown into a debtors' jail" (so Hugh Leonard reported in the *Sunday Independent*).

The Friends, however, were not primarily a Wood Quay group at the start but had an agenda of a broad range of topics affecting medieval Dublin. One of their first undertakings was the production of a booklet, compiled by Paddy Healy and Howard Clarke, detailing eighty-six medieval sites in Dublin. The group agreed to encourage archaeological work (but not engage in it themselves) by undertaking research which would be of use to anyone working on archaeological rescues in medieval Dublin. They considered applying for funds to the European Science Foundation; one of the uses of the funds would be the payment of artists called in to make emergency drawings of sewer cuts and other excavations in the medieval part of the city that were made without enough advance warning to call in an archaeological team.

The Friends made extensive recommendations to the city manager for inclusion of material on medieval sites in the forthcoming development plan. These recommendations were adopted almost in their entirety. The group also worked on the preparation for publication of two maps of medieval Dublin, one illustrated and one minutely detailed, both of which were published within a year, striking examples of cartography well up to the high standards of the Irish government's Ordnance Survey, which did the printing.

As the summer of 1977 drew near, the archaeological site at Wood Quay had been deserted for almost a year and the overgrowth was acceding to sylvan proportions. It occurred to Anngret Simms, then secretary of the Friends, that the deserted archaeological site was a potential medieval exhibit just as it stood. The Friends requested permission to open up the site to guided tours during the summer months and received cooperation from all concerned, from City Manager James Molloy, from Pat Russell, and from Joseph Raftery, who had succeeded Lucas as head of the museum a few weeks after the archaeological work on the site had ended. The Friends even received a £130 contribution from Dublin Tourism and a promise of £200 from Dublin Corporation's cultural committee to support the tours.

The tours began July 19, 1977, and were conducted Saturdays and Sundays throughout the summer from 11:00 A.M. to 7:00 P.M. Volunteers came in to clear the overgrowth, outline paths, build steps, and bridge the open cuts. Students were hired as tour guides or, rather, they took the jobs on speculation; they were told at the start that they would be paid if there was money to pay them, but there was no certainty that there would be money. They agreed to that arrangement and did, in fact, get paid at summer's end from the contributions left by visitors to the site.

An average of four hundred visitors a day took the tours. In the last weekends in August the number was around six hundred, and it happened several times that seven tours were on the site at once, and that the groups were almost too close for the guides to talk over each other. When the tours ended September 4, between seven and eight thousand people had gone through the site. The tour guides had been well versed in the excavations, there had been a lot to see, and the visitors came away enthusiastic about the medieval discoveries.

The last tour was Sunday, September 4. The next day the city council met and heard from Ruaidhrí O Brolchain, the deputy city manager, that construction on the civic offices was ready to recommence. This news was not a bolt out of the blue, for resumption of construction had been in the offing for months. Almost a year before, on October 4, 1976, the city manager had told the city council that the invitation of tenders (bids) for construction of the civic offices was being prepared and would be ready in two or three months. The city council's action accepting the deputy city manager's report at the September 5 meeting gave the firm of John Paul & Co., Ltd., the contract, which was described in the report as running for thirty months. Properly speaking this action was not resumption of construction, as it was popularly called, but initiation of construction.

Just as important as the council's approval of the construction was an amendment proposed by Alderman Kevin Byrne and passed along with the motion of approval: "That the Dublin City Council facilitate a small team of Rescue Archaeologists nominated by the Board of Works or the Museum to photograph and record the excavation which will take place while the building on the site is in progress." The idea is terribly modest—do you mind if we take a few pictures after the bulldozer goes by? But in fact this amendment helped put archaeology back in business on the site, for someone was going to have to come forward to do the photographing and recording. Reenter the museum (in a few months).

The irony, of course, was that fourteen months had been wasted. The museum could have been doing anything it wanted; the site had been served up to it on a platter. "The Wood Quay site has been vacant and available for excavation from July 1976," P. O'Muirgheasa, an assistant city manager, told the September 5, 1977, meeting of the city council.

In a telephone interview in July 1981 Dr. Lucas begged off answering any questions about Wood Quay on the grounds of his age, his health, and his fatigue over the whole business. Joseph Raftery, asked in an interview May 23, 1983, if the resumption of work at Wood Quay was the result of Kevin Byrne's motion in the city council to facilitate a small team of rescue archaeologists on the site, replied:

No, not really. I mean yes and no. Superficially yes. You see, you had a number of people who were using and exploiting the site for their own ends, personal advancement, self-enhancement, and so on. But all the time in the background with the powers that be, with the authorities in the corporation, with the Department of Education, with the Board of Works, we were trying quietly to get everything so organized that we would be able to go in and excavate. That was our—as I said—that was our one function, our one aim and that was what we believed to be our duty. But the job was made extremely difficult and was made particularly difficult for the men on the ground, because there was constant and daily interference from the, I call them, half-wits. . . . You see, when the work was going on on the old Dublin site, none of these people were ever heard of. . . . It was only when the thing became in some way fashionable that they all started climbing on the bandwagon. It was very interesting, a very simple piece of public relations. And it was, to use the Irish phrase, a certain amount of museum bashing.

Among the Friends and other Wood Quay advocates the news that the buildings were to go up created less of a stir than the news of where they were to go up. From the time that the three-area division of the site was worked out in 1974 it was assumed that the first building would be done on the north end of the site, in area 1. This, after all, was where the museum had begun working in 1974 and, important as the Norman finds proved to be, everyone knew that the south end of the site was older and richer. The logic of the permission granted to the archaeologists was that they should move on in advance of the construction, that is, southward, accomplishing all that they could before they had to relinquish successive areas to the builders. One statement after another from conservationists, e.g., an An Taisce press release of August 23, 1974, shows that this was an unquestioned assumption.

About a month before the September 1977 meeting of the city council word had come out that the two buildings to be built in phase 1 of the construction would not be the two on the north end of the site after all, but the two at the other end, where almost no archaeological excavation had taken place. The richest and most historically important part of the whole site, the main Viking area, was to be trucked out without archaeological investigation.

For the defenders of the archaeological work this was the most shocking development in the whole Wood Quay story to date. On August 2, 1977, F. X. Martin wrote to City Manager James Molloy to point out that the area to be cleared for the first two office buildings covered 700 square yards which had just become available for archaeological investigation as a result of the demolition of the building housing the turncock's office, 800 square yards next to that area with ten to twelve feet of habitation material, and 230 square yards on the south side of the site which had not been touched by archaeologists. He called for the establishment of an archaeological team to excavate ahead of the builders.

Sam Stephenson in an interview July 3, 1981, discussed the reaction to the news of where the building was to begin:

> I don't know what the reason was, but we ourselves were quite surprised when some of the medievalists said this was a change. It was always made quite clear to them that those were the first two buildings to go up, because underneath those buildings was planned and is planned what we call the energy center for the whole complex; the basic boiler rooms and all the service rooms of the entire complex are under the bigger block which is now beginning to go up. . . . So I never understood how they suddenly made this kind of jump as if this was kind of new. We never intended it any other way.

The "medievalists" are bound to ask when it was made quite clear to them that the two buildings to the south were to be the first to go up.

On September 5, 1977, F. X. Martin sent to Lord Mayor Michael Collins a plea signed by eight of Ireland's leading historians and archaeologists for "an adequate archaeological presence continuously on the site from the commencement of the clearance and building work." The immediate goal of this appeal was to affect the vote taken the same day the letter was delivered in the city council on the future of the site. As was mentioned above, the council did that day pass Kevin Byrne's amendment calling, more or less, for the "adequate archaeological presence" that the Martin document demanded.

There is a tincture of despair in even these appeals and resolutions, for there did not seem to be any real hope of retarding the building or accelerating the archaeology. But the protests, as they built up, became more confident. On October 4, 1977, a public meeting was called at the Mansion House by the Friends of Medieval Dublin to discuss the future of Wood Quay and the rest of the medieval city. This meeting was on the same order as the Mansion House meeting three years before organized by Deirdre Kelly and the Living City Group and was addressed by seven speakers who included F. X. Martin, Anngret Simms, Kevin B. Nowlan, Michael Herity, and

Liam de Paor, an archaeologist who had written a number of incisive newspaper columns on Wood Quay. At this meeting talk was bolder; five resolutions were proposed, among them a call for resumption of excavations at Wood Quay under professional supervision and with adequate time to complete the work in a scientific manner (in contrast to the onlooker's role that had been described in the council's September 5 motion). This was not enough for the audience, however, and another resolution was proposed from the floor and voted in: "The meeting expressed its strong opposition to any buildings on the Wood Quay–Fishamble Street site. The site should be preserved as a fitting monument to the history of our city." With that proposal in circulation, others like it began to be voiced in months ahead: enclose the whole area and leave the finds in situ, make Wood Quay a park after the excavation was finished, erect low-income housing on the site. See?—we told you, the corporation was able to say, they want to block the civic offices. And the argument mounted.

By November 1977 it was clear what the archaeological presence on the Wood Quay site was going to be. It was going to be the National Museum in the same force and under the same supervision as before, as if the team had never left the site in 1976. Funding had come through from the Department of Education for full-scale excavation, not just for surveillance.

Before the 1976 digs ended, some limited archaeological excavation had been started on the higher ground at the southern end of the site, although most of the team was working by the river right up to their last day. Pat Wallace had started a few workers on a plot near Fishamble Street in 1975, and it was near there that the first workers transferred by Breandán Ó Ríordáin from Christ Church Place in late summer 1975 began to work. When Ó Ríordáin finished Christ Church Place in January 1976 the remainder of his team came down to the Wood Quay site. Both of these excavations in the Viking areas, incipient as they were, had made some important discoveries before they were interrupted; the most important was that of the mudbanks already mentioned. They rivaled in importance the city wall and were, in fact, the city wall's predecessors. High, rounded banks built up of estuarine mud redeposited over wattle reinforcements and hardened like cement, they ran parallel to the stone city wall and south of it and were the earliest discovered fortification, the farthest from the river, of Viking Dublin. Their importance was clear to the archaeologists when they were found in 1975, but at that time they had barely been sampled. When the archaeological force returned to the site in the fall of 1977 the mudbanks had highest priority.

John Paul, Ltd., the construction company, had arrived a few weeks before the archaeologists; the builders' main activity in the vicinity of the archaeological area was the driving of sheetpiling along Fishamble Street preparatory to digging the fifteen-foot trench for the retaining wall. This was very close to the mudbanks.

Pat Wallace's first stratagem to protect the banks was to ask to have his huts set up practically on top of them. "I wanted to occupy that area so that the banks would be saved," he said. "I knew that the corporation probably intended bulldozing there. Just to secure the area I acted crazy and said, 'My huts must go in there.'" That ploy failed, for the corporation went to the trouble of concreting a base for the huts north of the wall. Then Wallace asked if he could put the spoil from his excavations in the area of the banks, knowing that that would kill the area. Here again he was refused.

For several days Wallace had seen the builders making test borings near the banks, and and then one day late in November, as he was laying out a site, he saw a bulldozer moving in on the banks. He ordered it to stop in the name of the museum. That succeeded for the day, but the director of the museum, Raftery, was in Germany and it was hard to tell how long the threat to the banks could be stayed.

Everyone on the site knew this, and word somehow got out. One of the Friends, speaking about other such occasions, said, "We several times got calls, sometimes even from the construction workmen, when something on the site was in danger." This may have been the first of those occasions, for the Friends knew about the danger to the banks within a day. The next working day was Monday, November 28, 1977. Early that morning F. X. Martin arrived at the site and appraised the situation. Within hours he was in court, and a whole new kind of battle was being waged over Wood Quay.

6. DLÍ AGUS CIRT

WHEN F. X. MARTIN appeared in the high court November 28, 1977, before Mr. Justice Declan Costello he asked, first, that the area of the Wood Quay site containing the mudbanks be recognized as a national monument and, second, that the Dublin Corporation be enjoined from doing further work on the site pending an outcome of the plenary action, that is, the request for national monument recognition. Justice Costello noted that it was unusual to make an order like the one sought without hearing the defendant, but because the danger was imminent and the destruction could take place the same afternoon, he granted an injunction valid only for two days.

When the National Monuments Advisory Council's standing committee met that afternoon, it agreed that there were national monuments on the site which were in danger of destruction, not merely the mudbanks but the stone wall and some wattle and palisade structures as well. The committee recommended a temporary preservation order and drew the attention of the Dublin Corporation to sections of the National Monuments Act forbidding destruction of a national monument.

The Irish may have heard more about national monuments in the media from November 1977 onward than they had since their school days. The question of whether or not Wood Quay or part of it was a national monument came to dominate the controversy over the site; the question was to linger in the courts for several years.

The key definition in Ireland's National Monuments Act, 1930, states:

The word "monument" includes any artificial or partly artificial building, structure, or erection whether above or below the surface of the ground and whether affixed or not affixed to the ground and any cave, stone, or other natural product whether forming part of or attached to or not attached to the ground which has been artificially carved, sculptured or worked upon or which (where it does not form part of the ground) appears to have been purposely put or arranged in position . . .

. . . the expression "national monument" means a monument or the remains of a monument the preservation of which is a matter of national importance by reason of the historical, architectural, traditional, artistic, or archaeological interest attaching thereto . . .

It might well be asked why the national monument question had not been raised sooner and by someone in an official position. Ireland abounds in national monuments. Throughout most of the country (but not very much in Dublin) one runs into them: megalithic tombs, castles, monastic ruins, forts, round towers, stone crosses, crannogs, buildings with distinctive histories. Some of them belong to and are under the care of city or county councils, but the majority are maintained by the National Parks and Monuments Branch of the Office of Public Works.

What the Board of Works could have done in the case of the mudbanks and other features of the Wood Quay site is the subject of some bureaucratic casuistry. In a strict construction of the law Wood Quay was not theirs to save, for the Dublin Corporation owned it, and the site's protector defined by law was the Dublin city council. Thus the Board of Works replied to the National Monuments Advisory Council's initial November 28 request for preservation of the monument that it was not the policy of the board to exercise powers conferred on it by Section 4 of the 1954 amendment of the National Monuments Act when the monument in question is owned by a local authority. Section 4 states: "Where it appears to the Commissioners [of Public Works] that a monument which in their opinion is a national monument is in immediate danger of injury or destruction the Commissioners may by order (in this Act referred to as a temporary preservation order) undertake the preservation of such monument."

The Board of Works was by no means the enemy of Wood Quay or of the national monument declaration. Peter Danaher, chief archaeologist of the National Parks and Monuments Branch of the board, was continuously involved in the effort to save the area of the Viking earthworks. He was a member of the National Monuments

Advisory Council and also of the council's standing committee, which did most of the council's investigative work into what was going on at the archaeological site.

The question was: were the three commissioners of the Board of Works enemies of Wood Quay? They were the real powers on the board and, as things worked out, the effective decision makers on the fate of the earthworks. They were John McCarthy, the chairman of the commissioners and a former head of the National Parks and Monument Branch, John Allen, and Sean Breathnach. Throughout the whole national monument controversy they enjoyed a near perfect anonymity, although press coverage of other aspects of the issue was constant and extensive. Their superior was the minister for finance, George Colley, who also held the post of tanaiste, the number two position in the government. Colley was assisted by a junior minister, Pearse Wyse, whose post was known at that time as parliamentary secretary (later changed to minister of state). On Pearse Wyse devolved the duty of making many of his department's public statements during the national monument controversy. On whom the ultimate decision making devolved, how independent the commissioners were of ministerial pressure, is hard to determine.

If F. X. Martin's request for national monument designation had been for a run-of-the-mill, uncontroversial site, a fairly simple machinery would have handled it. He could have submitted the request himself to the three commissioners or could have asked the National Monuments Advisory Council to examine and submit the request; the commissioners would have been free to accept or reject the request. Or the request could have been made through an alternate channel: a national monument may be declared by a local authority, that is, a city or county government. If the city or county happens to have, as Dublin does, a National Monuments Advisory Committee, that committee can forward its recommendations about the potential monument to the local government the same way that the National Monuments Advisory Council does to the Commissioners of Public Works. Many national monuments, moreover, are regarded as such without the benefit of formal designation; these are monuments which belong to the state or a local authority, are unthreatened, and do not need protective designation. Wood Quay could have been one of these, but since it was threatened, formal designation was the only way to protect it.

In November 1977 the National Monuments Advisory Council had thirty members including Joseph Raftery, A. T. Lucas, and Michael O'Kelly, who were aligned on one side of the Wood Quay battle, and George Eogan, Michael Herity, Liam de Paor, and Lennox

Barrow, who were on the other side. Lord Killanin, widely known for his presidency of the International Olympics Committee, was a member, as was E. Estyn Evans, director of the Institute of Irish Studies at Queens University, Belfast, and author of a number of absorbing historical-archaeological-cultural studies of Ireland. Breandán Ó Ríordáin was a member; Pat Wallace was not. The membership was varied and of blue-ribbon quality, and there was no question that the majority were in favor of protecting Wood Quay. Raftery resigned his chairmanship of the council in 1978.

The Dublin city council's National Monuments Advisory *Committee*—not the *Council*—met within five days of F. X. Martin's court action, requested reports from the Board of Works and the museum, and recommended a temporary preservation order on the site. The committee met several times again in weeks that followed and got nothing for its pains but a sheaf of perfunctory and evasive replies to its queries and recommendations. The corporation and the government had a way of treating the committee as if it did not exist. Later on it would be treated as if it existed—and shouldn't have.

It was a small body with a fairly limited mandate. The city of Dublin contains only a few declared national monuments (partly because a place of worship still in use cannot be declared a national monument). When the Dublin National Monuments Advisory Committee turned its attention to the restoration of Henrietta Street, in its day one of the most beautiful Georgian streets on the north side of the city, it got a sympathetic and cooperative response from the corporation. Wood Quay, however, was another story. One could chart on a graph the conversion of the city council to the Wood Quay cause from its early indifference to the site to its first unequivocally protective vote on May 4, 1979; through much of the earlier period the little National Monuments Advisory Committee was a convenient whipping boy for councillors who resented even the mention of Wood Quay in official business.

This reaction would probably not have been so strong if Kevin Byrne and Carmencita Hederman had not been on the committee— Kevin Byrne especially. An admirer of Saul Alinsky, Byrne was cunning, flamboyant, and unpredictable at council meetings. If time ran out on him when he was speaking on a motion, he would write out additional remarks in longhand, run downstairs to the corporation's copying machine, make forty-five copies, and return to the council chamber and hand them out. When he had done this repeatedly, he said, the city manager told him that he would be charged for the use of the machine. Byrne's answer was to photocopy the full *Oliver Twist* and present it to the city manager with the message that if he was charged for use of the machine, he would have the manager's books audited. When a key council meeting was moved to the Mansion House, Byrne packed it beyond capacity with his supporters by leading them to the door with the instructions, "Now stand close behind me and when I say, 'Stop shoving!' follow me in." He could turn a council meeting into a shambles—"I broke up five meetings in five years," he said—but it was always controlled and engineered disorder, never gratuitous.

His personal life is just offbeat enough to be in character with his public life. "I was a longshoreman," he said, "clothes designer, was in magazines and publishing, took a year off and drove a wagon and horses around. I lived in Cornwall, did some writing, was a potter in England. Came back to the university, got interested in town planning, went into the art business, ran a gallery. Then I went into schoolteaching and then politics. Then I became Adult Education Officer for Dublin, a new position."

Byrne's tactics, however, served a political vision which was more intelligent than his theatricality might suggest. A major part of the vision is the environment; he was a champion of environmental issues in the council, is a member of the Irish Council for Environmental Studies, and is anxious to bring in American experts to tool up Ireland's environmental programs. His use of a bicycle rather than a car to get around Dublin is intended as a dramatization of his environmental concerns.

While Byrne would probably not go quite so far as to call himself an "experienced archaeologist," as Carmencita Hederman suggested, he did in fact study archaeology for a year under the late Ruaidhrí de Valera. The year gave him some concrete knowledge of the science, and it also gave him an impression of the archaeological community, which he explained when commenting on the scarcity of support that he and Carmencita Hederman received from the archaeologists when they first brought up Wood Quay in the council:

> I suppose one of the problems with archaeologists is that there are so few jobs and they feel that if they open their mouths, they alienate themselves from getting on. The archaeologists with secure jobs in the universities are what Marx would have called free intellectuals in the middle, and they could have opened their mouths without fear of losing jobs or promotions. The reason that they didn't is that they come, like the priests in Ireland, from the most conservative of classes, farming, don't you know, small shopkeepers. People like that aren't going to stick their necks out.

George Eogan is one of the few archaeologists who comes out of
this whole thing smelling very well.

Byrne was probably the first Irish politician to realize that the
value of the Wood Quay finds lay not in their being a treasure trove,
but in their revealing the layout of the Viking settlement and the
pattern of medieval town life.

On November 30, 1977, when the two-day injunction expired,
F. X. Martin was back in court, this time with his adversary, Dublin
Corporation, present. An undertaking offered by the Dublin Corporation to do no more work on the site for two weeks was accepted; it
made continuance of the injunction unnecessary and postponed further argument of the case until the day the two-week undertaking
expired, December 14.

On December 14 Justice Costello made an order restricting the
corporation from work on the area of the Viking banks until January 6, 1978. The question of substance which he had to decide, he
explained, was whether the banks were in fact national monuments.
If they were, they could not be destroyed except in a way outlined in
Section 14 of the National Monuments Act, namely with the permission of the local authority, the Dublin city council, and the commissioners of the Board of Works.

On January 6 the high court sat again and Justice Costello
continued the injunction until the case could be heard and a final
judgment reached on the character of the banks. The corporation
immediately announced that it would appeal this decision to the supreme court.

On January 9, 1978, three days after the high court decision to
continue the injunction pending a full trial, the city council met and
voted on the report of its National Monuments Advisory Committee, which, as noted before, had recommended that a temporary preservation order be put on the area containing the Viking banks. Although this could have been a conclusive moment in the struggle for
the rescue of the site, for the city council legally owned the site and
had it in its power to declare the Viking fortifications a national
monument, no one would realistically have expected the declaration. The vote of 26 to 11 against the preservation order was a
barometer of the council's current feeling about the whole Wood
Quay issue.

When the Dublin Corporation's appeal of the high court decisions was heard in the supreme court on January 23, it rested mainly
on two planks, the harm done to the corporation by the injunction

and the *locus standi* of F. X. Martin, that is, his right as a private citizen to raise a question of public interest. The second plank was abruptly snatched away when Professor Martin's lawyers, Donal Barrington, Thomas Smyth, and Mary Robinson, announced that their client had been joined in the suit by Ireland's attorney general, Anthony Hederman, and that the plaintiff was now "the Attorney General at the relation of Francis X. Martin." No one could challenge the attorney general's right to raise a public interest question, but as the case proceeded it became clear that the attorney general's involvement was going to raise another question, that of his joint liability with his fellow plaintiff; this question was going to remain unanswered for several years.

The supreme court's response to the corporation's appeal came on January 25, 1978. It discharged the high court injunction in return for an undertaking on the part of the corporation to make no excavations in the defined crucial area without prior consent in writing of the Commissioners of Public Works and to allow archaeological excavations in the area as thought proper by the museum or the Board of Works. The case was then returned to the high court for a decision on the question of the national monument status of the area of the fortifications, the plenary action and the very first question which had brought Wood Quay into court two months earlier and which had still not been heard.

About a fortnight after the supreme court's decision—although it was not timed to relate to it—a witty tribute to Wood Quay appeared in the *Irish Times* in the form of seven sonnets on the archaeological site, the winners of that week's verse competition. This weekly competition, whose subject is announced a month and a half in advance, is one of the paper's popular features and draws, no matter how challenging the subject, contributions that give the myth of literary Ireland surprising credibility. The directions for the February 6, 1978, contest had called for a sonnet, after Wordsworth, on Wood Quay. First place went to Jack Bennett for:

> History had not uncovered quite so bare
> A memory of olden times until
> Chance bared these relics of time's grinding mill.
> Lo!—how through th' horizontal misty air
> Morn's oblique rays strike athwart, glinting where
> Christ Church's windows look, so pensive, still,
> In mullioned majesty down Michael's Hill
> On that sore quand'ry for the city's mayor.
> What wonder! What amaze! What ancient awe,

What else has all imaginations fired,
Or moves the mind to measure out in rhymes
These things now seen that Swift himself ne'er saw?
What else, oh after all, has quite inspired
So many letters to *The Irish Times?*

The day the sonnets appeared the city council met with some Wood Quay business on its agenda, the most important of which was Lord Mayor Michael Collins's motion "That the Dublin City Council consents to any excavation which may be necessary for the purposes of the construction of the Civic Offices . . ." The motion passed. The city council meeting ended with a vote, 22 to 13, of no confidence in the council's National Monuments Advisory Committee. The little committee just would not stop. Ben Briscoe, who proposed the censure, would rather have seen the committee dissolved, the *Irish Times* reported, but found that that was not feasible.

In March 1978 a forty-page report on the tourist potential of Wood Quay if it were developed as a public archaeological attraction was published. It was a sequel to a smaller report, both of them commissioned by the Irish Hotels Federation, and included a statistical examination of the tourist habits of visitors to Ireland and the volume of tourism at other centers of Viking preservation open to the public, namely York in England, Aarhus and Roskilde in Denmark, Bergen and Trondheijm in Norway, Hedeby in Germany, and Birka in Sweden. Known as the Colin McIver report, it was written by F. W. Roche and J. A. Murray of Colin McIver Associates (Ireland) Ltd. It described the character and appeal of the functioning tourist sites outside of Ireland, compared Wood Quay, and applied figures available on what tourists gravitated to in Ireland and what the annual growth rates in various forms of tourism were. The report concluded that Wood Quay, if opened to the public in a fashion comparable to the other Viking sites, would attract 100,000 visitors the first year and 300,000 per annum over a five-year period. A careful projection from records of spending of current tourists and the known motivations of attractable foreigners led to the conclusion that Wood Quay would generate at least £3.2 million per year in tourist revenue.

Throughout April 1978 last-minute preparations were being made for the state visit to Ireland of the reigning monarch of the land from which the Dubhghaill had come to Ireland eleven centuries before. Queen Margrethe of Denmark was to begin a four-day visit on April 24. On the queen's schedule were such classic functions as tree planting, a visit to a school, a tour of the passage graves at Newgrange, and a stop at the Waterford glass factory. What was conspicuously not scheduled for her was a visit to Wood Quay, which, according to secondhand reports, was one of the places she most wanted to see. It was not merely the Danish origins of the settlement that attracted her; she had studied archaeology at Cambridge University and had been quoted as saying that she would have been a professional archaeologist if she had not inherited the throne. It would have been hard to find anywhere in the world a head of state more interested in Wood Quay or a visitor more symbolically appropriate.

Predictably the refusal to let the queen visit generated more publicity than a press photo of her standing on the site would have. Kevin Byrne asked the corporation to request the Department of Foreign Affairs to extend to the queen an invitation to visit the site. And then Sean Loftus took action, and all other efforts to protest, capitalize on, or chortle gleefully over the queen's exclusion moved to the rear of the stage.

Sean Daniel-in-the-Lion's-Den Dublin Bay Rockall Loftus is without peer in the chambers of national and local government in Ireland. A mixture of Don Quixote, Machiavelli, and Francis of Assisi, Loftus belongs to no political party and has no permanent alliances in the city council, although his support of environmental issues and of the working-class poor finds him frequently voting with the same councillors, usually like-minded members from Labour, Fine Gael, or the independents.

He is a lawyer and law school lecturer with a special interest in planning law. He spent three years, he says, in the United States in the early sixties and while there met and was strongly influenced by Eduardo Frei Montalva, the president of Chile who had preceded and in many ways paved the way for the Marxist president Salvador Allende. Returning to Ireland, Loftus worked for several years as a community activist and tried to set up a Christian Democrat party guided by his impressions of Frei's political philosophy. He never succeeded in establishing the party except to the extent that he ran as its sole candidate in a city council election. Since party designations do not appear on ballots in Ireland and Loftus was staking much of his chance of election on the interest the new Christian Democrat affiliation would create, he went to court and changed his name to Sean D. Christian Democrat Loftus and so appeared on the ballot. It was not, however, until 1974 that he was elected to the city council and 1981 that he was elected to the Dáil. (One may serve simultaneously in national and local government in Ireland; Loftus is currently in the city council but not the Dáil.)

Part of his power comes from his unsettling combination of self-promotion and humility. His ego is prodigious, almost grotesque, like the traits of the heroes in the old Celtic tales, but it is solely at the service of his public functions. His political ambition is intense, his personal life almost selfless. He dresses as if sentenced to do so, but if election ever depended on dressing well, he would become a fashion plate overnight.

He is sincerely solicitous about his constituents and listens to them. He is kind hearted. On one occasion he ran across a street hurrying to an appointment, was struck by a car, and suffered a badly fractured leg; as soon as he was able to make a phone call from the hospital he called the woman who had been driving the car to assure her that the accident was totally his fault and that he would be all right. "Ah, she was terribly upset," he said. Not to waste gifts from heaven, however, he took advantage of the huge cast on his leg, once he was able to move about, by covering it with political slogans and walking up and down Grafton Street. So much free publicity came from this stunt that he failed to keep his clinic appointment when it was time to remove the cast and spent a few more days stumping with it.

He acts in defiance of the old axiom, *qui plura commendat fere nihil amendat*—anyone who makes too many recommendations ends up changing almost nothing—and sometimes succeeds in refuting it.

Energetic as he is in public relations, he is also bumbling. He releases sheaves of statements to the press, handwritten, photocopied, and nearly illegible. When deciphered they have a free-association air to them. The questions he asks the city manager at council meetings are rambling, prolix, and rhetorical. Copiousness casteth out logic in his methodology. Yet his techniques have worked for him probably more consistently than any others would have, and the issues that he champions, offbeat as they seem when he articulates them, turn out repeatedly to be crucial matters for the city and the state, which his more sober colleagues are soon forced to debate in their more sober manner. He is like a creature born without the organs normal to the species but endowed with others which compensate or overcompensate; they leave his movement erratic but his vision acute.

Two public issues had engaged Loftus particularly, and both sent him back to court for additional name changes. When fighting, on what turned out to be the winning side, the building of an oil refinery on Dublin Bay, he took Dublin Bay as his middle name. Later, when leading a battle to get the Irish government to pursue its claim against England to tiny Rockall Island, which lies in the Atlantic off

the Scottish and Irish coasts and is of value only because of petro-
leum exploration rights, he took Rockall as an additional middle
name. Christian Democrat was now dropped, but Dublin Bay caught
on with the public; newspapers and even the city council minutes
refer to him half the time not as Sean but as Dublin Bay Loftus. He is
greeted on the streets as Dublin Bay and he wears a button from the
old refinery battle, "Save Dublin Bay from Pollution."

Consistently opposed to building the civic offices on the Wood
Quay site, Loftus was one of the appellants against granting the
planning permission in 1971. He had made it clear that, although
he was concerned with saving the archaeological material, he was
at least equally concerned with having the civic offices relocated to
the north side of the city for the sake of improving that deteriorating area.

The Queen Margrethe episode was made to order for him. His
first move was to send the queen a packet containing photographs
and explanatory material on Wood Quay and a letter offering 100,000
welcomes (cead mile failte, the traditional greeting) and 100,000
apologies. The next move was to show up at the Mansion House reception for the royal couple with a bone given him by an archaeologist at Wood Quay. As Loftus tells it, "I held up the bone when the
royal party came out, and Prince Henrik broke rank and came over to
me to talk about it. I gave the bone to the head of the Danish press
corps. I asked my archaeologist friend later to give me another bone,
and this is the one I used with the media and others in New York and
Boston."

Loftus then appeared at Iveagh House (offices of the Irish Department of Foreign Affairs) with a wooden spoon from which a box
of matches was dangling. This he presented to the office of protocol
with a letter explaining the symbolism of the gifts; the wooden
spoon stood for the shambles that Foreign Affairs had made of the
royal visit, and the matches were for burning the spoon (presumably
in expiation). That was the essential Dublin Bay at work. The Danish
ambassador, he said, later wrote him at the royal command thanking
him for his concern.

The national monument question, which had been in the courts
for seven months at this point, was finally heard June 28–30, 1978,
in the high court before Justice Liam Hamilton. Every court action
up to this time had been merely temporizing—an injunction, an undertaking, an appeal—until the plenary question could be decided.
The testimony in favor of national monument status, especially that
of F. X. Martin, followed familiar lines—the uniqueness of the site,
the amount learned from it, etc. Ruaidhrí de Valera, professor of Cel-

tic archaeology at UCD, said that he considered the whole site, not just part of it, a national monument, just as the whole site at Tara was a national monument.

But the defendants had the most interesting witness. Professor Michael J. O'Kelly of University College Cork spoke against preserving the Viking earthworks. O'Kelly's reputation as an archaeologist rested on work at a number of digs in Ireland, none better known than Newgrange. Apart from Etienne Rynne, O'Kelly was virtually the only archaeologist that Lucas and Raftery were able to count on for public support. O'Kelly testified that other places in Ireland like Kilkenny, Wexford, Waterford, Cork, Limerick, and Galway were more useful sites for archaeological excavation. They would give a better view of medieval Ireland, and money would be better employed on them than if spent on "this hole in Dublin." Cross-examined on his choice of words (that day's headline maker) O'Kelly replied that he had heard the same expression applied to his excavations in Cork.

"By whom?" asked Donal Barrington, lawyer for the plaintiffs.

"Some of my Dublin colleagues."

O'Kelly said that discoveries on the site were repetitious, that all the work on the site could be finished by August, that is, in a month and a half, and that it was not feasible to preserve all the discovered timbers. "If you want to see what a Viking house looks like," he was quoted as saying, "build a Viking house."

Justice Hamilton visited the Wood Quay site in the course of the trial to familiarize himself, as he said, with the nature and extent of it. His judgment in the end was very narrowly phrased. It was to be conceded by all that there were monuments on the site and that the monuments were of historical, architectural, traditional, artistic, and archaeological interest. The only question was whether or not preservation of the site was a matter of grave national importance by reason of these interests. His judgment was that it was: the Viking fortifications and the surrounding area bounded by the city wall, Fishamble Street, John's Lane, and Winetavern Street constituted a national monument. The monument area, therefore, covered all the ground on which phase 1 of the civic offices was to rise. This was the first time that *dlí agus cirt*, the legal process, had made a national monument declaration in Ireland.

7. JOINT CONSENT

THOSE WHO wanted to could express their pleasure at the court's decision. It was natural for the Friends of Medieval Dublin to do so, but they knew better than anyone else that they had probably won a pyrrhic victory. The headline in the *Irish Independent* read, "Court rules in favour of Wood Quay fighters, but—." The "but" was the fact that national monuments could be destroyed. All that was required was the joint consent of the local authority, in this case the Dublin Corporation, and the Commissioners of Public Works.

Everyone involved in the case knew—and the defenders of Wood Quay naturally advertised the fact—that, in spite of Section 14 of the National Monuments Act, no authorization had ever been given to destroy a national monument in Ireland. So there was a kind of moral injunction, it was bravely argued, against destroying this one. On July 4, 1978, four days after the verdict, the city manager wrote to the Commissioners of Public Works asking "That they would join with the Corporation in giving consent under Section 14 (2) of the Act to demolish and remove wholly the National Monument subject to the preservation of the old City Wall and such other conditions (if any) as may be agreed."

The commissioners' response came on August 2:

> The Commissioners . . . not having yet had sufficient time to decide on its [sic] final position in regard to the Corporation's request, has requested the Corporation to allow archaeological excavation and investigation by the National Museum to proceed on the Site for the period from the 31st day of July, 1978 to the 28th day of August 1978 (both dates inclusive) to which the Corporation has agreed.

The rest of the document was a formal joint consent not for the corporation to demolish the monument as requested but for the museum to excavate with the proviso that the city wall—and the earthen banks—not be touched.

The National Monuments Advisory Council's standing committee had visited the site before and after Judge Hamilton's verdict, had met with Pearse Wyse, minister of state for finance, on May 30, 1978, and had sent its recommendations to the Commissioners of Public Works on July 19. On August 25 Wyse issued a statement announcing that the August 2 joint consent to allow archaeological excavation until August 28 had been extended by six weeks, at the end of which time the corporation would be free to proceed with the building of the civic offices "unless some new archaeological find of great importance has been made"; he added that in reaching this decision the Commissioners of Public Works had adverted in particular to the advice of the standing committee of the National Monuments Advisory Council.

The NMAC replied in a September 8 letter to the commissioners regretting the decision and complaining that Wyse's statement gave the erroneous impression that his decision was in accord with the thinking of the council. An Taisce on August 31 also replied in detail to Wyse's statement, noting the unreality of the clause, "unless some new archaeological find of great importance has been made."

How little in accord Wyse and the NMAC were came out when the fortnightly *Hibernia* published on September 21, 1978, the unreleased report of the NMAC to the Commissioners of Public Works. (*Hibernia* was at the time the best organ of investigative journalism in Ireland; it was mature and lively and too effective a lightning rod for libel actions to stay long in business. Nothing has quite taken its place, although the current level of investigative reporting in *Magill*, *In Dublin*, the *Sunday Tribune*, the *Irish Times*, the *Irish Independent*, and, to some extent, *Hot Press*, *Phoenix*, and *New Hibernia* is good, Ireland's reporters have long complained that they are kept so constantly on assignment that they do not have time for the investigations they want to pursue. A reporter at the *Irish Press* said one day, "I just met an American reporter in London—he was over for two weeks working on a story. Can you imagine? Two weeks!")

What *Hibernia* readers saw was this set of recommendations from the NMAC to the Commissioners of Public Works:

(1) That consent should not be given under Section 14 (1, 2, and 3) of the National Monuments Act, 1930, for any actions which would lead to the demolition of any part of this Monument or the destruction of archaeological evidence;

(2) that there should be a phased archaeological excavation of the site, designed to recover the fullest information;

(3) that consideration should be given to the permanent conservation of the Monument and its environs.

It was clear that the positions of Wyse and the NMAC were irreconcilable.

While the conflict between these two authorities was making news, a document that should also have been making news was signed and sealed on August 29. It stated in part:

> AND THEREFORE the Commissioners and the Corporation in exercise of the powers vested in them jointly by virtue of section 14 of the National Monuments Act, 1930 Hereby Jointly Consent and Agree that the Corporation as owner of the said National Monument as defined by the said Order of Mr. Justice Hamilton and shown bounded by a green line on the Map hereunto annexed may by itself its Servants or Agents Demolish and Remove Wholly or in Part and may otherwise interfere with, excavate, dig or otherwise disturb the ground within, around or in proximity to the said National Monument to the extent necessary to permit the completion of the said recited Contract for the erection of the said Civic Offices on the Site. . . .

This was *the* joint consent, the death sentence on the archaeological site. It was the paradoxical, virtually inevitable conclusion to the court action that F. X. Martin had undertaken. Was there a strong reaction to the signing of the joint consent? There was no reaction at all, for almost no one knew about it. Not only was there no public knowledge of it when it was signed and sealed, but there was no general knowledge of it through the rest of 1978. During this time the Wood Quay advocates, the National Monuments Advisory Council, the city council, and, for a second time, the courts devoted themselves with new urgency to the business of Wood Quay, all of them either in the dark about the consent or unaware of its force. That such a key official document in such a controversial matter could escape public attention for over four months will seem either freakish or scandalous.

When the fact of the joint consent became general knowledge, a storm of wrath broke over the head of Pearse Wyse, the minister of state on whom responsibility for the joint consent devolved by virtue of his office's oversight of the Board of Works. Wyse was angrily accused of concealing the joint consent, and the accusations stayed alive for months. On March 13, 1979, Wyse used time in the Dáil to answer the charges of concealment against him.

In the long run it would be too much to say that Wyse comes out of the matter without a leg to stand on. He comes out with one leg. In his March 13 Dáil speech, Wyse offered two defenses: (1) his public statement of August 25, four days before the joint consent, was an announcement of the consent, and (2) the consent was announced at the city council meeting of September 4, 1978, six days after it was signed. The first defense is not sufficient; what Wyse said on August 25 was an expression of the intention of the government: "When the [remaining six weeks'] excavation is completed, unless some new archaeological find of great importance has been made, the Corporation will be granted permission to proceed with the building of the Civic Offices." It may be argued that this implies that a joint consent is on the way, but such expressions of intention, often enough amended or discarded, had been part of official utterance about the Dublin archaeological sites almost from the beginning of the work and were not taken seriously unless it was clear that they promised to have results.

Wyse's other argument, that the consent was announced at the September 4, 1978, city council meeting is substantially correct. A report was presented by the deputy city manager and recorded under "Lord Mayor's Business" that excerpted the most important part of the six-page joint consent; the report was subsequently printed in the minutes of the meeting. One councillor said it was "washed through" on courtesy to its submitter as a number of unexamined reports and breviates are at most council meetings; Andrew McHugh, administrative officer of the Dublin Corporation and probably the best authority on the council's minutes, said that the notes kept for the purpose of preparing the minutes of the meeting indicate that the statement was read to the meeting. In any event the council's usually vigilant defenders of Wood Quay seem to have been asleep at their posts the night of that meeting, and the joint consent crept through the chamber with its coat collar turned up, went out into the night, and was not seen again for four months.

Memories of the event have grown dim among officials and activists alike. It seems likely that the Wood Quay defenders were lulled into inattention by the avalanche of official documents on the civic offices. The term *consent* had begun to be used on permissions to continue the archaeological work, e.g., the April 18, 1978, letter from the Commissioners of Public Works to the city manager consenting to fifteen additional weeks of archaeological excavation on the Wood Quay site. And the joint consent to destroy the monument also contained an extension of six weeks for additional archaeological work.

It was really quite extraordinary. What the government would have done if someone had pounced on the joint consent and published it can only be guessed. But since no one did, the following interesting calendar took shape: on November 23 Wyse met with the NMAC and told them that no decision had been made about the site. On November 28 Wyse gave a speech in the Dáil about his responsibility to consider all viewpoints before making a decision about the site. In his December 7 speech in the senate Wyse spoke mainly about the difference between excavation and preservation. In his December 8 meeting with the NMAC Wyse discussed a variety of Wood Quay subjects—the museum proposed for the basement of the civic offices, the wall, the amenity of the area, questions of preservation—but not the joint consent. In the December 19 meeting with the NMAC and others, Wyse spoke about a new development on the site, the southern retaining wall. But not the joint consent; always the impression remained that the final decisions were yet to be made.

When the attacks against Wyse mounted, he was able to get off the hook by citing the one occasion on which the joint consent had been made public. But the question remains, since the joint consent was one of the major events in the whole history of Dublin archaeology, why did not Wyse himself or an appropriate corporation spokesperson voluntarily bring it up? It would have been in place in all the speeches and meetings just named, especially the meetings with the NMAC.

Three things in particular stand out during the period of the joint consent's latency: increasing protest, progressive sensitivity to Wood Quay on the part of elected officials, and a new threat to the monument (from a source other than the joint consent) that was going to send F. X. Martin back to court for another injunction.

First, there was protest: there was a meeting attended by two thousand people at the Mansion House on September 14, 1978, and there was a march through the streets of Dublin September 23. The overflow meeting resembled the 1974 and 1977 Mansion House meetings but the speakers' emphasis this time was on appeals to the taoiseach, the minister for finance, the Dáil deputies, and the city councillors.

The September 23 march, announced well in advance, was an extravaganza that attracted between 17,500 and 20,000 people and people from a wider variety of backgrounds than had palpably been part of the Wood Quay protest before. The marchers, who assembled in Kildare Street in front of the government buildings and the National Museum, included union groups, elected officials, residents' groups, schools, academics, other organizations, and the general public. Many of the marchers were in Viking costume. Thomas Kinsella, the poet, led the march, Senator Mary Robinson spoke at one of the stops, letters of protest were dropped off at the National Museum, the Board of Works, and city hall, and a letter of appeal was left for the taoiseach. The march snaked through the streets to the sound of pipers and bands in a line like a big question mark—Nassau Street, Lincoln Place, Merrion Square, Hume Street, St. Stephen's Green, Grafton Street, Dame Street, and Wood Quay. Scheduled to arrive simultaneously with the marchers at Wood Quay was a replica of a Viking ship in the Liffey. The march had been well promoted in advance, but its size was still surprising. It made it difficult for politicians to refer any longer to the Wood Quay activists as "a bunch of middle class trendies from Dublin 4." It did not make it impossible for Professor O'Kelly of Cork to speak of "the Father Martin lunatic fringe rent-a-crowd."

Two of the most spirited press commentaries on the march came from *Red Patriot* and *Hot Press*. The former, the news weekly of the Communist Party of Ireland, published a flyer for distribution at the march, which said in part:

> This militant demonstration of opposition to the government's plan to destroy Wood Quay is a reflection of the universal sentiment of Irish people in defence of the cultural heritage of our nation. . . . The struggle to defend the working people's historical heritage is an important part of the overall struggle to take our destiny in our hands and rid ourselves of the parasitical imperialist system and its agents, the native monopoly capitalist class which is the cause of the exploitation of our people and the destruction and abuse of our environment and the root of all the problems that the Irish people face.

Hot Press is Ireland's counterpart of *Rolling Stone*. F. X. Martin described it with undue avuncularity as "the highly popular weekly paper of the irrepressible teenage music lovers." The irrepressible teens get to read some of the most incisive journalism in the country. *Hot Press* on Raftery:

> Dr. Raftery has appeared to be equally willing to let the site go the way of all flesh, uttering a series of strange and seemingly paranoid statements—on TV he certainly gave the impression of be-

lieving that the whole public protest was being orchestrated by a bunch of people who were out to embarrass *him*, in particular.

On the inability of lower-level museum officials who criticize the museum policy privately to speak out publicly about it:

> . . . if civil servants were allowed to speak out on what they saw going down, not only would you have a far more efficient bureaucracy, but you would even have some intelligence and honesty in government.

And in the final analysis:

> The plain fact is that our asses are in the grip of nincompoops and cretins. The only answer is massive doses of public cynicism and aggression towards our blockhead government. . . . And if anyone wants a justification for going to the streets on the matter, aside altogether from the huge intrinsic qualities of the site, and its discoveries, and its potential for tourism, and for insight into the Irish people, that's it. The question of showing who's boss. Of course there's also the fact that Vikings are more fun. It's like rock 'n' roll. (*Hot Press*, October 6–20, 1978)

Galvanized into action by the march, the government as a whole gave Wood Quay some attention. The cabinet met on September 26, 1978, three days after the march, and directed the Commissioners of Public Works to agree to additional time for archaeological excavation. On October 10 the commissioners complied and allowed the museum an extension up to December 9. (The significance of the October 10 date is that the permission previously in effect expired October 9. That permission was given in the still virtually unknown joint consent.)

On October 5 the standing committee of the National Monuments Advisory Council visited the site and recommended that the state take it over from the corporation and guarantee a properly phased, unhurried excavation. On November 10 the standing committee visited the site again and immediately wrote to the commissioners expressing dismay at what it saw. Excavation, its letter said, was proceeding at much too great a speed and in piecemeal fashion. Again the committee urged a properly phased excavation.

At its October 2, 1978, meeting the city council defeated, 28 to 8 with 1 abstention, a motion by Dublin Bay Loftus to move the civic offices project to the north side of the city, but two months later on December 11 when the Labour group in the council presented a long motion, the most important part of which was a proposal that the civic offices be moved to that part of the Wood Quay site which was not a national monument and had already been excavated down to bedrock (i.e., north of the city wall), the motion lost by only one vote, 19 to 20.

A few days before the latter vote in the council, the Wood Quay issue was raised on the national level when the senate debated a motion by Senator Gus Martin, well-known member of UCD's English Department, calling for an indefinite preservation order on the national monument. Ireland's senate does not have power comparable to the Dáil's, but its debates on occasion bring major controversies into focus. This motion was Wood Quay's moment in the senate and was debated for two days, December 6 and 7; the motion lost 21 to 20 to the disappointment of the Wood Quay lobby, a disappointment rendered more poignant by a vote against the motion by Senator John A. Murphy, of Cork, whom the preservationists had more or less counted on, and the absence from the chamber when the vote was taken of Senator Mary Robinson, whose vote was certainly counted on.

Popular support for the archaeological cause grew during 1978 both in Ireland and in foreign countries. In January *In Dublin* magazine, which is an Irish counterpart of *New York* magazine, ran a signature campaign calling for full archaeological excavation of the site. Early in the campaign the magazine notified the taoiseach of 12,000 signatures received. Later in the year the Friends of Medieval Dublin ran their signature campaign and announced receipt of 210,000 signatures. Prestigious foreign scholars signed petitions which were published in the Irish papers. The Friends of Medieval Dublin put together a three-page list of Irish organizations offering their support. In November, when the corporation devoted an issue of a newsletter published periodically for use in the schools to a flashy presentation of the new civic offices with the corporation's apologia for the buildings, some schoolteachers refused to distribute it.

The unions were generally supportive of the Wood Quay cause. One union that was not was the already referred to Local Government and Public Services Union, headed by Harold O'Sullivan. This was the union that represented the corporation office workers in the city's then dispersed offices. It would be hard to deny them their grievance; some of the corporation's offices—the Planning Department, for example, in the Irish Life Center—were modern and attractive, but others makeshift and cheerless, good film locations for stories about Kafka's civil servants. On at least one occasion the charge was made that if there was strict enforcement of the city's sanitary and fire codes, some of the civic offices would have to be shut down. With these conditions on the one hand and fantasies of things to come created by pictures of Sam Stephenson's luscious office towers on the other hand, it is not hard to see why LGPSU turned out for a march of its own a few days after the big march of September 23. About five hundred union members left their desks to parade in support of the civic offices.

The new threat to the national monument which came at the beginning of 1979 was a surprise to the Wood Quay defenders and looked as if it had a good chance of succeeding; it was an effort to remove the national monument in the name of safety. The day after New Year's Day 1979 the builders began mechanical work preparatory to erecting a concrete retaining wall around part of the south end of the site almost on top of the area in which the archaeologists were working. This area, known as the cliff area after the high cliff face created by the earlier mechanical excavation described in Chapter 1 (which by cutting down through the rich archaeological material had created a *tranche des âges* in which the strata of successive centuries could be pointed out), was also the area of the mudbanks and other unexcavated deposits.

The already standing protection against subsidence of the earth in the area was sheetpiling driven into the earth down to boulder clay well below the level of archaeological interest. The sheetpiling paralleled Fishamble Street from a point near the old city wall and then curved to the west as it neared Christ Church cathedral. Inside, that is, north of, this sheetpiling worked everyone on the site, archaeologists and builders.

According to a statement made by City Manager Molloy to the city council January 8, 1979, the corporation had learned a month earlier on December 4, 1978, that structural engineers were concerned with safety on the site. C. H. Clifton, an engineer, advised the erection of a retaining wall comparable to the one built beginning in 1974 on the north end of the site at the expense of a roughly fifteen-foot margin lost to archaeology around the perimeter. The "free standing materials adjacent to sheet piling" which Mr. Clifton said would have to be removed for the building of the wall were the archaeological soil at the south end, the oldest and richest part of the site. In other words, the national monument.

Molloy further informed the city council that at the December 19, 1978, meeting of the corporation, the chairman of the Commissioners of Public Works, the NMAC, Pearse Wyse, and Raftery, he had told those assembled that the corporation in the light of the reported danger had no option but to proceed with the remedies advised. "No one," he went on to say, "at the meeting opposed this line of action." Whatever was said at the meeting, "this line of action" was opposed right after the meeting by the NMAC, which wrote to the minister for finance reaffirming what it had said in its report to the commissioners in July 1978, namely, that it wanted phased archaeological excavation—not demolition, but preservation of the monument.

After a day's preparation the bulldozers were ready to move. They leveled a raised square of land near the cliff which the archaeologists had not finished excavating. On Thursday, January 4, 1979, when the archaeologists arrived for work at 8 A.M., they took positions in front of an important part of the cliff to prevent any of the excavating equipment from getting at it. That maneuver worked for the day; while the archaeologists were doing sentry duty, the cabinet was meeting. Wood Quay was on the agenda, but the agenda was not completed, and there was no discussion of what was going on at the site. That night members of the archaeological team stood watch through the night.

The watch continued through the weekend. On Monday the eighth the archaeologists held a meeting at 8:30 in the morning and agreed to prevent further mechanical excavation unless the builders could present a license allowing them to destroy the national monument. About half an hour later one piece of earthmoving equipment started work on a trench through unexcavated ground. The archaeologists stood in the trench, and work stopped. Pat Russell was on the site, but Pat Wallace was away for a few days, and Raftery did not appear until later in the day. Two of the young women working on the site questioned Pat Russell about his authorization to break Section 14 of the National Monuments Act. "First, you're archaeologists, then engineers, and now lawyers," Russell said. One of the site assistants went up to the Board of Works to inquire about the authority of the corporation and was told that the work under way was needed to retain the sheetpiling and that the commissioners of Public Works had agreed that this was necessary. When the working day ended four or five of the archaeological staff stayed on the site to keep watch until dark.

During the day several people off the site had been heard from: Dublin Bay Loftus had asked the taoiseach to relocate the offices, Pearse Wyse said that he had given his recommendations about the civic offices to the government but would not say what they were, and, most important, F. X. Martin informed the city manager that he was applying for an injunction to protect the national monument. Word of the new court action spread through the archaeological team and heartened its members.

The next day, Tuesday the ninth, there was no mechanical excavation until the archaeologists took their tea break at 10:30. Then they noticed that one of the machines had been started up and that a driver was headed for another. Two of the site assistants jumped onto the first machine's bucket. "Keep her going," shouted one of the John Paul bosses, "dig like hell." But the driver did not keep going. The archaeologists then told the foreman and the machine operator that an injunction was being taken out and that they risked being in contempt of court. Pat Wallace was still away from the site, and Nick Maxwell was acting as an unofficial spokesman for the staff. Raftery and Russell informed him that all archaeological excavation was suspended owing to lack of an excavating license. The archaeologists stopped working, assuming that the builders would also cease work, but confrontations continued through the day. The machine operators did succeed in removing two or three bucketloads of archaeological soil.

On Wednesday, January 10, 1979, Justice Hamilton, the same judge who had made the national monument declaration, granted a temporary injunction good for six days forbidding Dublin Corporation from interfering with the national monument without the joint consent of the Commissioners of Public Works. On January 5, when they knew nothing of the joint consent, reporters had asked Pat Russell whether the retaining wall was not just a "back door" into destruction of the monument. "Totally untrue," Russell said. If the reporters had known, as they soon would know, that there was in fact a front door, unlocked and ajar, into demolition of the monument, Russell would have been questioned more closely.

The joint consent was eventually revealed. Why had it not been used? If the national monument had simply been destroyed by those now authorized to destroy it, no one would have cared whether new retaining walls or anything else was built on the site, and the corporation would not have been dragged into court again. The easiest inference is that the joint consent was the nerve gas of the Wood Quay war—there was no way to use it without admitting that it existed, and that was apparently the most distasteful admission that the corporation and government could have been called on to make.

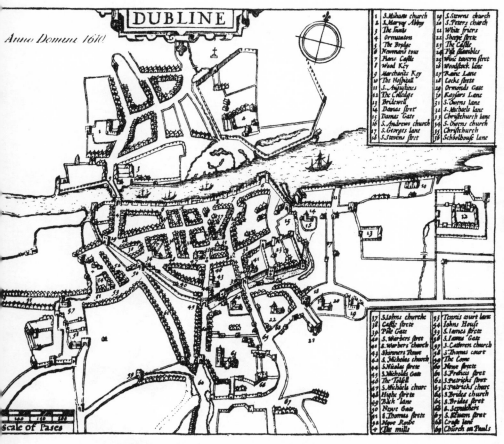

John Speed's 1610 map of Dublin, showing many vestiges of the medieval town. Wood Quay ("Key") is no. 8 in the center of the map; Fishamble Street is the Fish Shambles (no. 24). Originally published in Speed's *Theatre of the Empire of Great Britaine* (1611); reproduced in Anngret Simms, "Frühe Entwicklungsstufen der europäischen Seehandelsstädte . . . ," in *Lubecker Schriften zur Archäologie und Kulturgeschichte*, vol. 5 (Bonn, 1981); courtesy of Anngret Simms.

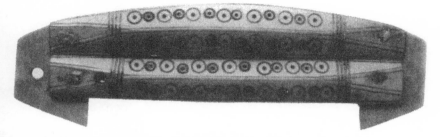

Eleventh-century polished antler comb case from Viking Dublin excavations.
Photo: National Museum of Ireland.

Opposite page: John Rocque's 1756 map of Dublin showing the city as it was around
the time of the death of Swift. The streets are close to the present street plan. Pud-
ding Row west of Wood Quay no longer exists, and the only remaining trace of
John's Lane between Christ Church and Wood Quay is a paved walk that is part of
the civic offices' landscaping. Composite map from 1756 original, from Anngret
Simms, "Medieval Dublin: A Topographical Analysis," *Irish Geography* 12 (1979):
28; courtesy of Anngret Simms.

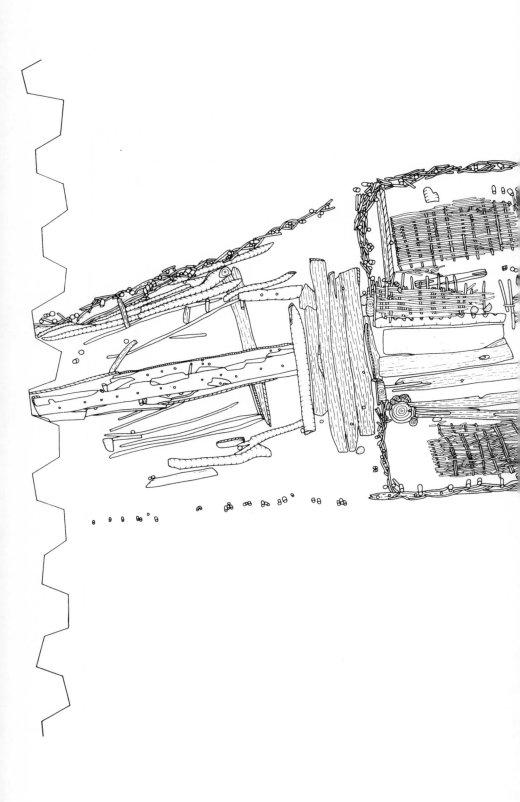

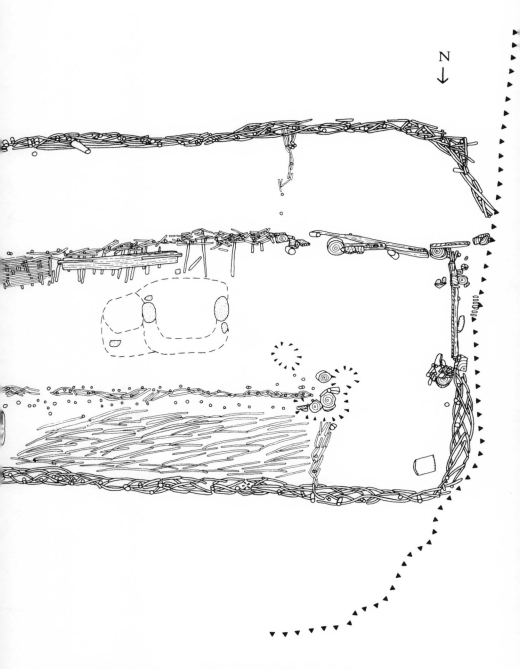

Plan of one of the eleventh-century houses, Fishamble Street. The central hearth and the corner posts placed well into the room are typical of the Norse houses found at Wood Quay. Drawing courtesy of the National Museum of Ireland.

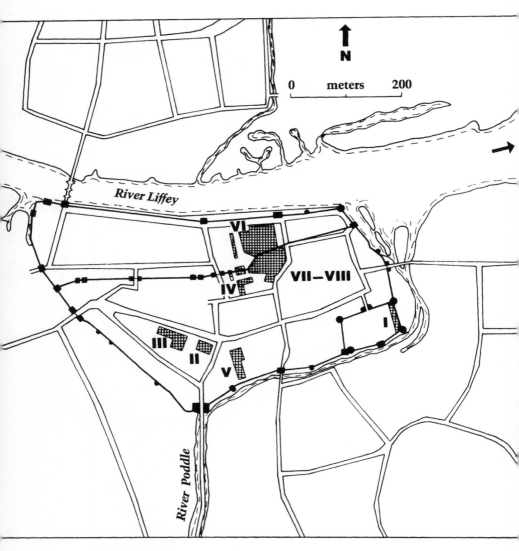

The locations of the Dublin archaeological excavations, 1961–1981, on a map representing the features of the medieval city. The river Poddle entering from the south now runs underground, and the Liffey is now much narrower than shown here. The excavations are: I, Dublin Castle, 1961; II, High Street One, 1962–1963; III, High Street Two, 1967–1972; IV, Winetavern Street, 1969–1973; V, Christ Church Place, 1972–1976; VI–VIII, Wood Quay, 1974–1981; (VI, the Norman area; VII–VIII, the Fishamble excavations). Map by John Bradley.

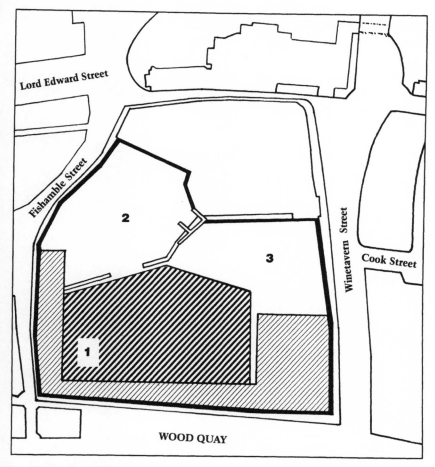

The three-part division of the site agreed to by the Dublin Corporation, the architects, and the National Museum in 1974 stipulated that the museum would have nine months to excavate in area 1, two years in area 2, and three years in area 3. The earth in the lightly shaded area running around from Fishamble to Winetavern was removed without archaeological excavation to construct a retaining wall. Adapted from map provided by the *Irish Times.*

Overleaf: Aerial view of the Wood Quay site in 1980, looking toward Christ Church Cathedral and the south. The Liffey is at the bottom of the picture. The Viking wall can be seen dividing the site from east to west; the two bends creating the "dog leg" are in the center of the site. North of the wall, nearer the river, is the Norman area; south of the wall, toward Christ Church, is the Viking area, on which the civic offices were built. Near the bend in Fishamble is the area in which most of the Viking houses were found. Photo by D. L. Swan.

NEWSLETTER

Dublin Corporation Schools Newsletter   Issue No 44 Nov/Dec 1978

A New Museum for Dublin

Sam Stephenson, architect of the civic offices.

When the Dublin Corporation Schools *Newsletter* appeared in November 1978, containing the corporation's twelve-page defense of the civic offices and its handling of the Wood Quay site, some teachers refused to distribute it. The cover is the architect's rendering of a medieval museum promised for the basement of the civic offices; no such museum was built. Courtesy of Dublin Corporation.

Helen Lane, an architectural student at Bolton Street College of Technology, Dublin, records the post-and-wattle breakwater at the north end, the Norman area, of the Wood Quay site, March 1975. Behind her a wide swath of archaeological material is dug up by a construction excavator clearing land for a retaining wall. Photo: *Irish Times.*

Section of an early-thirteenth-century wooden waterfront in the Norman area of Wood Quay. Photo: National Museum of Ireland.

Thirteenth-century post-and-wattle groyne or breakwater on the north side of the Wood Quay site. Photo: National Museum of Ireland.

Joining the September 23, 1978, march. Photo: Eddie Kelly, *Irish Times.*

Overleaf: Twenty thousand demonstrators gather on Kildare Street to march on the Wood Quay site September 23, 1978. Photo: Paddy Whelan, *Irish Times. Inset:* Alderman Kevin Byrne coming from city hall in full robes to join the march found the iron gate in front of the building locked. Photo: *Irish Times.*

An overview of the site in the middle of November 1978 showing archaeological excavations going on around the remains of more recent building foundations. A month and a half later the corporation argued that safety considerations required the construction of a retaining wall on the edge of the site and began bulldozing for it. The archaeologists stood in front of the bulldozers to block them. Photo: *Irish Times.*

March 8, 1979: One day after the supreme court permitted destruction of the national monument, the construction company's excavators remove the soil, rich in Viking remains, in the southeast corner of the Wood Quay site. Photo: Pat Langan, *Irish Times*.

Six thousand marchers move through the center city toward the Wood Quay site, March 31, 1979. This demonstration followed the march of twenty thousand protesters on the site seven months before. Photo: *Irish Press*.

Lord Mayor Carmencita Hederman; as an alderman she was one of the first members of the city council to draw attention to the importance of the Wood Quay site and to question the corporation and the National Museum about dangers to the archaeological resources. Photo: Billy Mooney.

Occupiers of the Wood Quay site hold one of the gates, June 1979. Mary Lavin is seated with her back against the gate in the center of the picture, partly concealed by Richard Haworth (with beard); Bride Rosney (white button on her jacket) is two to her left. Photo: *Irish Press*.

Two occupiers try to save their Viking raven flag, the symbol of the seizure of the site, from an attack by the crane operator, who had just succeeded in tearing down the Old Dublin Society banner. Dermot Walsh climbed up the outside of the crane structure and disabled the crane with a wooden peg. Photo: *Irish Press*.

Sean Dublin Bay Loftus, right, talking with Tony Collins, a fellow occupier of the Wood Quay site, June 1979. Photo: Jean Mattson.

Left to right: Gemma Hussey, later Ireland's minister for education; Sheelagh Richards, Abbey Theater actress; and Mary Lavin during one of the more relaxed moments of the occupation of the Wood Quay site, June 1979. Photo: Jean Mattson.

Trinity College (not Balliol) student Brid Ni Craith occupies a generator in preparation for the return of the construction workers. Photo: Jean Mattson.

The day after the occupation ended F. X. Martin looks down on the Wood Quay site from a window in the Casey house, 26 Fishamble Street, one of the command posts of the occupiers. Photo: Peter Thurfield, *Irish Times*.

Overleaf: Excavating the Viking houses along Fishamble, March 1980. In this area was found the largest collection of houses and house plots in all of the Dublin excavations; they shed substantial new light on Norse and medieval Irish architecture. Photo: *Irish Times*.

Workers on the Wood Quay site dismantling the numbered stones of the Viking wall without the supervision of archaeologists, around the beginning of October 1980. Photo: Pat Langan, *Irish Times*.

Two members of the archaeological team examine the skeleton of a young person found on the site March 22, 1981. The next day the excavations ended permanently. Photo: Jack McManus, *Irish Times*.

An archaeological assistant working on drawings in the midst of the Fishamble houses, May 1980. Photo: Paul Goulding, *Irish Times.*

Evening view of later-twelfth-century house foundation remains in the Fishamble area of Wood Quay. Photo: National Museum of Ireland.

Opposite page: Eleventh-century crook or walking-stick handle (?) carved in the Dublin version of the Hiberno-Norse art style known as Ringerike; found on the Fishamble part of the site. Photo: National Museum of Ireland.

Pat Wallace examining some of the Wood Quay finds in the basement of the Merrion Row annex of the National Museum of Ireland. This room, the largest single repository of Wood Quay material, contains many rows of cases like the above to house the finds, which Breandán Ó Ríordáin has numbered at more than a million. Photo: Shay Lattimore.

The civic offices in 1988 shortly after they were opened for business; Christ Church in the background. Photo: T. Heffernan.

The Viking wall as it runs underneath the rear of the civic offices, 1987. Photo: T. Heffernan.

8. EMOTIONAL TERMS AND SECTION FOURS

HE ACTION that F. X. Martin took in the high court led to an interlocutory injunction against the corporation on February 12, 1979, and the setting of a trial date. The corporation hoped that it could appeal to the now disclosed consent to definitively justify its destruction of the monument. The revised argument of the plaintiffs, however, focused first on the precise conditions set down in the consent and second on what it charged was the inaccuracy of the corporation's claim that the retaining wall was necessary for purposes of safety.

When the August 29, 1978, consent was given, it qualified the sweeping permission to destroy the national monument with four conditions, one of which called for more excavation time "if the investigations and excavations by the National Museum should result in some new archaeological find of great importance," and another for the museum to be given "facilities to inspect and record finds of historical or archaeological interest in the manner provided in the said Building Contract." The provision in the contract referred to was a clause in the bill of quantities which stated among other things that "the Contractor shall take all precautions to prevent his workmen or any other persons from removing or damaging any such [archaeological] articles or things and upon discovery thereof and before removal shall immediately acquaint the Architect of such discovery . . ."

In the light of the richness and density of the archaeological deposits on the site, strict observance of this clause would have turned the construction workers into archaeological assistants. The clause, however, did not become public knowledge until it was disclosed during the trial.

On January 26, 1979, George Eogan, Michael Herity, and Peter Danaher of the NMAC inspected the site and two days later swore an affidavit that they had observed the destruction of archaeological material including parts of at least two boundary fences of post construction, elements of the site which, "with the house sites, pathways and enclosing banks are the most significant structural features of the site and are of great archaeological importance."

Nicholas Maxwell, Pat Wallace's unofficial second in command and spokesman for the archaeological assistants on the site (and editor of *Digging Up Dublin*, a short book on the Dublin excavations), writing to the *Irish Times* in a letter published March 31, 1979, was more detailed about what was found on the site:

> . . . that area was approximately 440 square yards and approximately 12 ft. deep. It contained at least three earthen banks, one of which was the earliest yet found in Dublin, a number of houses, at least two pathways, and was the richest source of stratified artifacts on the whole site. The area also contained two burials, both of which had remnants of hair and one of which had a brain intact.

When the question of the need for the retaining wall arose, the plaintiffs presented an affidavit sworn by Peter McCabe, an engineer experienced in sheetpiling and soil containment work, who concluded, "I am of the opinion that the present retaining wall is over structured in every respect in other words more than strong enough and is unlikely to yield or fail . . ."

Although Justice Seán Gannon, when granting his interlocutory injunction on February 12, had set a trial date, the corporation did not wait for the trial but appealed at once to the supreme court. The appeal was heard from March 1 to 7, 1979. Chief Justice Thomas O'Higgins, writing the verdict, found in favor of the corporation and dismissed both the interlocutory injunction and the plenary action. His reasoning on the main points of argument was, first, that the Commissioners of Public Works were under no obligation to advert to any professional advice before signing the consent, and, second, that the extra time called for in the consent, should objects of great archaeological value be found, applied only to time which might be required for the treatment of those objects themselves. Noting that since the execution of the consent 1,500 objects had been found on the site, Justice O'Higgins said, "It has not been suggested nor could it that more time was required to investigate any one of the 1,500 objects found."

The legal score was now one and one. F. X. Martin had been successful in his first recourse to the courts and unsuccessful in his second. This case, like the one before it, was a relator action, that is, a joint suit, with the attorney general. When Justice Gannon, on February 12, 1979, granted an interlocutory injunction forbidding the destruction of the national monument, he required an undertaking, that is, a guarantee for damages, against F. X. Martin but in terms that led to some contention in court at a later date—the question was whether the undertaking given covered only the period of the first interim injunction in the case or whether it stayed in force throughout the case. The question of undertakings for damages was further complicated by the attorney general's being a plaintiff in the case; the judge explicitly noted that no undertaking would be required of him. When the corporation appealed to the supreme court, Justice O'Higgins threw out the injunction obtained in the high court and also dismissed the plenary action. On March 11, four days after the supreme court judgment, F. X. Martin announced that he was bringing the decision to the European Commission of Human Rights in Strasbourg, seeking relief under Article 25 of the Convention for the Protection of Human Rights and Fundamental Freedoms. His application to the commission in Strasbourg rested on the alleged denial of justice caused by the supreme court's dismissal of the plenary action. The corporation's appeal before the supreme court, Father Martin stated, was properly limited to the injunction only and was so argued by his attorneys; the plenary action would in the expected course of events have been returned to the high court for hearing. The supreme court, Father Martin argued, erroneously decided that it had the consent of both parties to embark on a consideration of the substantive questions of law in the plenary action and in doing so made findings "which were either contrary to the evidence, disputed in evidence, or related to matters on which I had been denied an opportunity to call witnesses and to adduce evidence because of the interlocutory nature of the proceedings."

On May 8, 1985, the European Commission of Human Rights found Father Martin's application inadmissible on three grounds, the most important of which was that any claim that fair hearing had been denied would have to pertain to determination of the individual's own "civil rights and obligations," which was not the case in the *actio popularis* that Father Martin undertook: he was seeking by his suit to protect the public interest, not his own personal rights; therefore his case did not fall within the provisions of Article 25 of the Convention appealed to.

The corporation announced in July 1979 that it was going to seek to recover costs of £200,000 from F. X. Martin and the attorney general. On February 11, 1981, Miss Justice Mella Carroll found F. X. Martin alone liable for damages and rejected the corporation's view that the attorney general was liable. The significance of this judgment for the corporation was that it could seek to collect only from a mendicant friar with a vow of poverty and no estate, while it could not collect from the attorney general, from whom some substantial recovery could have been made. A public concern was that a verdict against the attorney general in this case would have effectively discouraged the attorney general from entering public interest suits as a relator in the future.

The corporation was unwilling to abide by the high court's exclusion of the attorney general from liability and took the question to the supreme court, which on February 16, 1983, upheld the high court's judgment that F. X. Martin was liable and the attorney general not liable.

On June 7, 1984, an agreement in court between Dublin Corporation and F. X. Martin set Father Martin's liability at £89,500. The most discussed aspect of the case even before the June 1984 figure was announced was how F. X. Martin with his vow of poverty and a salary as a history professor which he turned over in full to his order was going to pay any costs assessed against him. He has paid nothing to date. Noel Carroll, announcing the corporation's resolve to collect, was quoted in a Dublin paper as saying, "It's not a question of anything but A owing B money, and he cannot do a Pontius Pilate on it . . ." There followed booing and hissing from the stands.

It was around six o'clock in the afternoon when F. X. Martin and his lawyer, Mary Robinson, left Justice O'Higgins's court and walked the few hundred yards to the Wood Quay site. "We came out of court and saw the bulldozers, . . . a lovely sight," Mary Robinson said later with a bitter laugh. F. X. Martin at once issued a statement to the press charging the corporation with violation of the condition of the consent which called for provision of facilities to the National Museum to inspect and record finds of archaeological value; none of the museum's archaeological team was on the site while the work was going on.

By noon the next day the bulldozing was finished. Noel Carroll, who with other corporation officials had begun to favor a little catchphrase, "Bulldozer is an emotional term," answered the charges that the museum was not in on the work as the consent required. The *Irish Times* quoted him as saying that there was no archaeologist that he knew of on the site during the excavations. Dr. Raftery, he said, had been consulted the night before about the archaeological aspects of the work and it was "the business of the National Museum where its staff was. There is no way the work proceeded without the imprimatur of an archaeologist."

Even though the cliff area was lost, there was still much to save on the site. The question that the Friends of Medieval Dublin and the other activists weighed now was how best to do that. The only answer seemed to be one kind of political pressure or another.

A natural opportunity to use political pressure was provided by the upcoming elections in June 1979, which would fill all forty-five city council seats—the term is five years—and choose Irish delegates to the European Parliament. The European Parliament is not yet taken too seriously in Ireland, but a number of Irish politicians are anxious to get elected to it for the sake of forming or joining international caucuses on issues like the environment which they are particularly interested in. The European Parliament could—and in fact did—offer one more source of international pressure on the Irish government's Wood Quay policy. The important elections, though, were the city council elections. By March 17 the Friends had launched their campaign for and against candidates for the council on the basis of their Wood Quay record. John Healy, whose column in the *Irish Times* sometimes brings Jimmy Breslin to mind, prophesied that Wood Quay would bury the predominantly anti–Wood Quay Fianna Fail, but most observers were unwilling to guess just how widespread support for Wood Quay was among the people as a whole. By the end of May campaigning was in full swing for the June 7 elections.

The city council then in its last months was no lame duck, for most of its members were running for re-election. During April and May 1979 the council took up Wood Quay business at several turbulent sessions. At the April 2, 1979, meeting of the council Dublin Bay Loftus and three other councillors introduced a Section 4 motion to relocate the civic offices.

A Section 4 motion (which takes its name from Section 4 of the City and County Management [Amendment] Act, 1955) is the most powerful weapon in the ill-stocked arsenal of local democracy in Ireland. The first effect of a Section 4 motion is that it is put first on the agenda, which is often left unfinished at council meetings. The second effect of a Section 4 motion is that it may oblige the city manager to do something, provided the something is legal and fundable. The Section 4 motion is sometimes the only way for the city's elected representatives to take control of the local government away from its appointed officials.

Loftus's Section 4 motion, which came down to a proposal that the civic offices be relocated on the north side of the city, had some publicity before it came up in the council. In a March 15 letter to the *Irish Times* he explained that he had tried to have the same motion passed the year before but lacked support. He felt that he was now at

the point where he needed the support of only eleven more councillors to have his motion passed. The letter appealed to the public
to urge their own councillors to support the motion. Loftus added, "I
asked the organisers of The Friends of Medieval Dublin's great march
to tell the thousands of marchers what to do next—to, as individuals, get their friends to lobby the Dublin City Councillors to support
my motion. They refused; evidently they didn't want to get involved
in the politics of Wood Quay either!"

By and large everyone in the Friends of Medieval Dublin liked
and admired Sean Dublin Bay, but it was inevitable that something
less than a perfect meeting of minds should prevail between them.
On both sides were fairly strong egos thoroughly convinced that
they knew the best way to go about things. Neither wanted its strategy changed by adaptation to the other's. On Loftus's side there was
a feeling that the Friends were too academic and on F. X. Martin's
side a feeling that Sean was too antic. Nonetheless, Loftus's letter
went on to say:

> I have two other Wood Quay motions coming up for decision on
> April 2nd—one, that Father Martin not be sued by Dublin Corpo-
> ration, (there are precedents for this sort of thing) and, two, that
> Dublin Corporation indemnify Father Martin for his costs, dam-
> ages, etc., and that because Wood Quay is a national issue, Dublin
> Corporation asks the Government to indemnify it.

The inclusion in the same letter of his complaint about betrayal, as
he saw it, at the hands of the Friends and his championing of F. X.
Martin at a time when talk was spreading of Father Martin's impending liability was not just for political effect but was the working of
his irrepressible fairness. It is always hard to bring Sean into focus.
He is a rare serpent and dove.

When Loftus's Section 4 motion was presented at the council
meeting, the lord mayor, Paddy Belton, a rotund and prosperous pub
owner, ordered a statement from the corporation's law agent read. It
said in part, "This Motion amounts to a direction to the City Manager to stop the building of the Civic Offices. To do this would in-
volve a breach of the subsisting Contract between the Corporation
and John Paul Ltd., and is thus illegal." William Dundon, the law
agent, often advised the council. Everything he told them about
Wood Quay business had the air of keeping the children in line. His
opinions were so supportive of the city manager and so disciplinary
of the councillors that Kevin Byrne asked at one council meeting, "Is
he your law agent or ours?"

Paddy Belton ruled the Loftus motion out of order and called for further business. "At this stage," read the minutes of the meeting,

> Councillor Dublin Bay-Rockall Loftus and Alderman K. Byrne left their seats and objected strenuously to the Lord Mayor's ruling. When they continued to disregard his request that they resume their seats and cease interrupting the business of the Council, the Lord Mayor at 6:45 adjourned the meeting for ten minutes. At 7:04 p.m. the meeting was resumed. . . . At 7:09 p.m. because of further grave disorder created by the same two members of the council the Lord Mayor declared the meeting adjourned to Monday, 9th April, 1979 at 6:54 p.m.

When the lord mayor left his seat, Kevin Byrne ran up and occupied it, announcing, "As the meeting is over and the lord mayor is gone, we'll hold our own meeting. I'll be a good lord mayor." The community councillors and the public gallery stayed on, criticizing Belton's conduct of the meeting and discussing what to do next. Outside the chamber Belton encountered about a hundred spectators. "A crowd of bowsies [riffraff]," he called them, the *Irish Times* reported.

When the council next met, a week later, there were a few of the gardai (police) in the chamber. Loftus said to one of them as he went in, "If there is trouble and you need a hand, I'll help you carry that big fat slob out." There was trouble. Loftus rose to request consideration of the motion ruled out of order at the last meeting. "Paddy turned off my microphone again," Loftus said. "One of the corporation officers, the corporation secretary, kept conducting business and the council responded to him all the time that Paddy and I were shouting. I didn't object to that; I didn't want any building contracts held up." That meeting broke up too. Loftus would have gone to the high court to compel the lord mayor to allow debate on his motion if he could have afforded the costs. He asked the Friends to stand the costs, but they declined. A fundamental difference, as Loftus saw it, between him and the Friends was that the Friends had confidence in the growing sympathy for Wood Quay in the ranks of Fine Gael and the Labour Party in consequence of which they would be ready to accept building on the north end of the site if archaeological excavation of the south end were allowed. Loftus felt that the Friends' trust was misplaced and that it had to be all or nothing, no building at all on the site.

The months following the supreme court decision were another one of the uncertain interludes which had punctuated the Wood Quay work from the start. On March 29, 1979, there had been an-

other meeting at the Mansion House, and on March 31 another siz-
able march. Support continued to come in from foreign and Irish
sources. The Wood Quay advocates were especially buoyed by a resolution of the Parliamentary Assembly of the Council of Europe in
Strasbourg supporting the city council's 22 to 15 vote for renegotiation of the contract and re-siting of the buildings.

It was during these days, too, that schoolboys found a Viking
sword on a dump to which the corporation had been trucking the
material excavated in the wake of the supreme court decision. An
official of the Irish Society of Antiques, Arms and Militaria was
quoted as saying that a similar sword auctioned in Christie's two
years before had brought £10,000. Joseph Raftery was out of the
country at the time, but in an interview with Frank McDonald of
the *Irish Times* an unidentified museum official said that when the
corporation was determined to go ahead with the building on the
Wood Quay site the museum chose as the lesser of two evils to have
the mechanically excavated material dumped at a Board of Works
site in Islandbridge, for even though its context was destroyed the
material could be sifted for finds. The greater of two evils would
have been dumping the material in the sea. Noel Carroll was quoted
as saying, "Who were the school children who found this sword and
who are the museum authorities who are making statements these
days, since the director, Dr. Raftery, is out of the country? Do they
have the authority to make these statements?"

To judge by some statements in the press during March and
April, there was growing dissent from the museum policy within the
museum itself. In a letter to the *Irish Times*, published March 17,
1979, fifteen members of the faculty of University College Cork, representing history, archaeology, geography, and literature, wrote:

> It is clear that the building of the Dublin Civic Offices on this site
> is to go ahead despite the fact that the professional archaeologists
> in the National Museum who carried out the actual excavations
> disagree with the officially expressed opinion of that institution
> regarding its preservation. It will be appreciated that this is highly
> unusual, if not unique, for public servants to openly disagree with
> the official opinion of their office, and we would, incidentally, like
> to compliment these scholars on the courage and integrity which
> they have displayed in doing so.

In his letter to the *Irish Times*, published March 31, 1979, Nicholas
Maxwell wrote, "It is well known that *all* the staff of the National
Museum find Dr. Raftery's approach to Wood Quay an embarrass-

ment." In an April 4 article in the same paper, John Bradley, of the department of archaeology at University College Dublin, wrote:

> . . . it is clear that all of the archaeologists in the National Museum oppose both the Corporation and their own director (Dr. Raftery) on the issue. Dr. Raftery is there in a minority of one. It was established in the recent court case that the entire archaeological staff of the Wood Quay site, employed by the National Museum, opposed the Corporation policy. Further it was also established that the entire archaeological staff of the Office of Public Works also oppose the Corporation case. It is in fact the case that no single Dublin-based archaeologist has supported Dr. Raftery on this issue.

As the elections drew near, the Wood Quay activists turned to campaigning, but the outcome of the elections was something that the Friends did not allow themselves to be unduly optimistic about and, from all appearances, that the corporation did not allow itself to be unduly pessimistic about.

The elections, however, were not the only thing coming. During the preceding months, as far back as December, several prominent and several not particularly prominent Dubliners who were interested in saving all that could still be saved at Wood Quay got phone calls from F. X. Martin. Would they be interested in doing something? *Something* was not explained to most of them. They would be told more shortly and in the meantime were to say nothing of the conversations. It was time for *something* new.

9. UNDER THE RAVEN

THE MAIN entrance to the Wood Quay site, both for workers and for heavy equipment, was halfway down Winetavern Street. Winetavern becomes, for no evident reason, quite wide at that point. Across from the archaeological site Cook Street comes to an end at Winetavern; it is the street that follows the line of the old city wall and which, if not interrupted by the site, would lead into Essex Street on the Fishamble side. The view up the hill to the south from the corner of Winetavern and Cook streets is dominated by the arching Victorian stone passageway which bridges Winetavern and connects Christ Church cathedral with its synod hall on the west side of the street. Between the synod hall and Cook Street on the west side of Winetavern lies a car park obviously created by the leveling of buildings.

Farther north on Winetavern between Cook Street and the quays, and facing the quays, stands Adam and Eve's, better known to the readers of the opening words of *Finnegans Wake* as Eve and Adam's ("riverrun, past Eve and Adam's, from swerve of shore to bend of bay . . ."). This large church, outwardly unimpressive but on the inside striking for the subtle tones of its wall colors, covers the ground on which in the seventeenth century a little alley, Rosemary Lane, ran between Merchants Quay and Cook Street. From Rosemary Lane one could enter a pub named Adam and Eve's, and from the pub one could enter a secret passageway that led to the rear room of a house on Cook Street. In this room during penal days Catholics gathered surreptitiously for mass celebrated by a Franciscan priest, until the house was raided and seized in 1629. When in the eighteenth century the Franciscans returned to the area they founded a church on Merchants Quay to which they tried to give the name Immaculate Conception—unsuccessfully, for everyone knew that the church was heir to the pub, and to this day its name is Adam and Eve's.

Every working day, now that legal obstacles to construction

work at Wood Quay had been removed, the workers passed in and out a small door in the plywood walls on Winetavern; one of the construction company's supervisors kept his car on the site, and for him the wide gates were swung open and closed. Around 6:40 P.M. the last of the workers trickled out of the site and moved up the hill to High Street or down to the quays. They were followed by the foreman in his car. Then the night watchman locked the gates to the street and unlocked the door of a kennel, releasing two Alsatian watchdogs which had the run of the four acres until the next morning.

A little after 6:00 P.M. on Friday June 1, 1979, a handful of men wandered into Adam and Eve's and stood in the back of the church. Services were going on at the time, and several friars and lay people noticed the group, some of whom were carrying hammers and most of whom seemed vagrant and suspicious. Seeing that they were being watched, the members of the group drifted out of the church and gathered again in the car park on the west side of Cook Street, joined now by a priest and a nun. A garda car drove down Winetavern and slowed as the driver caught sight of the group. The priest smiled and waved cheerily, and the garda waved back and drove on.

Across Winetavern Street the workers left the site; Monday would a be a bank holiday, and they were looking forward to the long weekend. A few minutes after 7:00 the wide gates opened, and the foreman's car crept up the graded ramp from the lower level of the dug-out site and appeared at the gate. The group across the street had been watching the car and had been watching even more closely a window in the top floor of a house at 26 Fishamble Street which was in line with the car straight across the site. As the car came level with the street, a white towel fluttered out the window of the house on Fishamble. At that signal the group in the car park, joined by a man who had been sitting nearby in a car, ran toward the gate and squeezed past the two sides of the car, saying to the astonished watchman, "This is a peaceful protest."

F. X. Martin and Dr. Margaret MacCurtain stood a short distance inside the gate, one of the group ran to the kennel and put an additional padlock on it, and the others—Richard Haworth, John Gallagher, Leo Swan, Seamus O'Reilly, Seamus Kelly, Aidan Dunne, Michael O'Brien, Kevin Byrne, and Sean O'Maonigh—collected to confront the construction people. As it turned out, there were four of John Paul's people on the site—the watchman, the driver of the car, a workman who had stayed behind to use the loo, and John Paul's chief of security, who had been making a periodic inspection of the site. Apart from calling the gardai, none of the construction men seemed to know what to do.

Their confusion was increased when they discovered that the little band that had burst through the gate was only the first wave of trespassers. Although four of those who had entered were prominent Dubliners, the group to come was the celebrity contingent. Around 7:30 a parade came down the hill from the direction of Christ Church which included poet Thomas Kinsella; novelist James Plunkett; Mary Lavin, the country's leading short-story writer; Alderman Alexis Fitzgerald; George Eogan; Senator (later Minister for Education) Gemma Hussey; Denis Larkin, a labor leader who might be described as the George Meany of Ireland; Donal Nevin, then assistant secretary and later general secretary of the Irish Congress of Trade Unions; sculptor Oisin Kelly; Michael Scott, prominent architect; and Michael O'Leary, at the time deputy leader of the Labour Party and a member of the Dáil. One squad car had already arrived as the second wave entered the site; no effort was made to stop the demonstrators. Alexis Fitzgerald recognized the garda in the squad car as one of his campaign workers.

In a matter of minutes Operation Sitric, as the takeover had been named by its organizers (after a Hiberno-Norse king of Dublin) had succeeded. It was, as *Hibernia* observed a few days later, "no half-assed amateur affair." It had been long in the planning and had remained, against considerable odds, a secret.

F. X. Martin was the author of the operation. Close to him in its planning were some familiar Wood Quay activists and a few people not yet prominently associated with the cause. The most important of the latter were Bride Rosney, a teacher and school administrator from Malahide, and John Bradley of University College Dublin's department of archaeology.

One member of the break-in who had been for some time publicly recognized as an advocate of the archaeological cause was Richard Haworth. A product of Queens University, Belfast, a former employee of the state-sponsored planning and research body, An Foras Forbartha, he was at the time of the occupation the geographical librarian at Trinity College. He had become known for his Wood Quay articles in the *Irish Times, Town and Country*, and elsewhere.

Another member of the occupation, Michael O'Brien, heads a major Irish publishing house, O'Brien Press. During the occupation he became a kind of Odysseus on the plains of Troy. If the occupation had allowed room for a little guerrilla activity, no one would have enjoyed the prospect more than he. "I think there is some Russian in him," said Richard Haworth, a kindred spirit.

Margaret MacCurtain, a well-known Dominican nun and cousin

of Siobhan McKenna, was a lecturer in history at UCD at the time of the occupation. She subsequently became principal of Ballyfermot Senior College, an institution whose student body and modern physical plant suggest an American community college, and which under her direction was innovative in curriculum and firmly anti-sexist in policy. She has left the college and is once again a faculty member at UCD; she is also coeditor of Gill and Macmillan's paperback history of Ireland series and was for several years head of Arlen House, a pioneer women's press. She is known on appropriate occasions as Sister Benevenuta, O.P., and it was in her avatar as a Dominican nun that she showed up for the break-in at Wood Quay. "I keep a habit hanging in the closet for occasions like that," she said.

John Gallagher is the head of the Liberties Association, a quintessential neighborhood association. The Liberties lie south of Wood Quay, west of St. Patrick's cathedral, and east of Guinness's Brewery—more or less: as the Liberties have become fashionable, a number of Dubliners have laid claim to having been born there or having grown up there, which claims occasionally seem to stretch the boundaries. The Liberties are as authentic a working-class neighborhood as can be found in Dublin. The modest plastered row houses are built out to the narrow sidewalks. Suggestions of poverty are everywhere, but the houses are well maintained and the neighborhood is clean. There is a pride of place among the residents, even a consciousness of the neighborhood's medieval origins (an area of special administrative privilege outside the city walls and not subject to the city charter, whence its name). Recent years have witnessed what could be the first stage of gentrification of the area as media people and creative types have discovered the charm, centercity convenience, and low real estate prices of the small Liberties houses.

John Gallagher is the neighborhood's public advocate, unofficial social worker, legal aid society, recreational organizer, and counselor. Talking to him in the make-do headquarters of the Liberties Association, one thinks of Dorothy Day and the Catholic Worker (neither of which Gallagher had heard of). He is informed, practical, and usually cool when he analyzes and participates in local politics, but at times the wrongheadedness or massiveness of an injustice sends him into a rage.

He said that he had three reasons for joining the Wood Quay occupation: the site was a national monument, the neighborhood would be damaged by the large offices, and the view of Christ Church would be blocked. But as he talks it becomes clear that there was another reason too: he saw the Wood Quay protest as a rare display of democratic action cutting across categories of Irish citizens, and he hoped that it would be the beginning of an enduring democratic activism reaching into other areas of Irish life.

Both the "task force," as the first wave of occupiers called themselves, and the celebrity contingent had assembled in the afternoon in the Pious Union Hall, a building connected with a large Augustinian church on Thomas Street. The vantage point from which John Bradley waved a tea towel as a signal to the first occupiers was the fourth floor of the Casey house on Fishamble Street. The Caseys are a family of campanologists—they ring peals in the city's bell towers—who formed a lively and committed Wood Quay underground, offering the view from the fourth floor parlor of their house, which was the only remaining residence on Fishamble and which, Mrs. Casey claims, had been in their family since the eighteenth century, to F. X. Martin's band before the occupation and to the press afterward. Earlier, at the time of Queen Margrethe's unsuccessful effort to visit Wood Quay, Mrs. Casey had hung a Danish flag from a window where it could be seen from the site.

The gardai responded in force but did not attempt to expel the occupiers. Some workers who had returned to the gate when they saw that something unusual was going on demanded to be let back in the site to get their tools, but were at a loss to do anything about the invaders. Bride Rosney quoted one of the construction company men as saying that if the police did not get the occupiers out, he was going to the bishop. A Sean O'Casey line. Reporters and photographers arrived. The only paper notified in advance had been the *Irish Times*, whose editor, Douglas Gageby, sent Caroline Walsh to cover the story; the reporter did an open-mouthed double take and exclaimed, "Mother!" when she saw Mary Lavin among the occupiers.

Inside the site the occupiers assembled at the base of the city wall to hear Tom Kinsella read a proclamation, which among other things charged that the period between the last meeting of the old city council and the first meeting of the new was a governmental vacuum in which destruction of the site was proceeding at a rapid pace. He called for the cessation of all building work during the interregnum between councils. This was one demand that was going to be granted, not through concessions from the corporation, but because the occupiers were going to hold the site throughout that period, something which none of them would have been ready to predict.

Another of the demonstrators who spoke, Kevin Byrne, said, "If we are really aware of what it means to be Europeans, we should know that it's not just a question of getting money from the Social

Fund. Membership of the EEC has duties as well as rights." This strain of exhortation had become increasingly common as the events of Wood Quay unfolded. "You're European now!" was one of the reminders directed at the Irish by continental commentators on Wood Quay ("now" meaning since Ireland had joined the European Economic Community). The whole idea will seem curious to Americans—of course the Irish are European, what else?—yet in many ways the Irish enjoy a remarkable detachment from European thought, European problems, and European trends, as if the island sat somewhere between Iceland and the Azores, a mid-Atlantic nation. Irish writers discussing the national mind repeatedly comment on this isolation.

Supplies were moved onto the site. A large tent was set up inside the main gate, and a rented caravan, or house trailer, was parked across Winetavern in the car park to serve as a public information center. The occupiers changed a lock on one of the gates and braced the other closed with posts; they opened the museum's huts and moved all the artifacts and archaeologists' equipment which had been left into one of the huts and took over the others as sleeping quarters.

The flag of the occupation, painted by Kay Doyle, F. X. Martin's sister, after an old Viking symbol, was a black raven on a white ground. It had been raised Friday night over a Nissen hut inside the main gate. In the middle of the night three bold lads decided that the raven should be flying from the top of the construction crane, the highest point on the site. They detached the flag from the hut and started up the crane. When they were noticed, a group of horrified watchers gathered below. The three climbed up into the darkness and disappeared from sight; it was only with the help of lights the gardai supplied that they could be followed. Finally the task was abandoned; first the raven came floating down to earth, then, grip by grip, came the would-be flag raisers.

The site was patrolled through the night by the occupiers who had drawn duty for that shift. Around 5 A.M. they heard hammering on the wooden walls around the site. Investigating, they found a woman from Sean Loftus's campaign staff nailing election posters along the fence, proclaiming the site Loftus's election headquarters. The message from the occupiers was that the site was not his headquarters and that the posters were not welcome. The angry worker left and returned a little later to accuse the Friends of once again betraying Loftus, her anger apparently fueled by Saturday morning's *Irish Times*, which had just come out carrying two pictures side by side on the front page next to the news of the occupation; one was of F. X. Martin looking through the fence, the other of Michael O'Leary, who was an opponent of Loftus's in the European elections, looking over the fence. In the minds of Loftus's supporters it was bad enough that Dublin Bay had not been told about the occupation and asked to join it and that Michael O'Leary, who at the time had a rather man-about-town image and had never had any conspicuous relation to the Wood Quay cause, had been asked to participate, but it was worse that Martin and O'Leary were pictured together, creating the impression that F. X.'s support was going to O'Leary.

F. X. Martin's answer to the complaints of Loftus's supporters is, in essence, "Why not?" Michael O'Leary was a rising star. He was not only a power in the Labour Party (which he has since left for Fine Gael) but seemed destined for a role in any coalition government that might oust the then reigning Fianna Fail machine. It was practical politics to back O'Leary, quite practical, as it turned out, for in two and a half years O'Leary was tanaiste, number two man, in the coalition government headed by Garret FitzGerald. Loftus himself is not the grudge-holding type; for that one turns to his brother Paddy, a sometime campaign aide, who is close to turning what he sees as the Friends' betrayal of Sean into an epic.

Loftus himself heard of the occupation from one of his campaign workers who, he was told, had been phoned by Caroline Walsh. As Loftus tells it, he at once canceled a campaign appearance that he had scheduled in Terenure and went to the site. The occupier at the gate thanked him for coming, Loftus said, but did not let him come in. Loftus asked why he had not been informed and invited, but felt he was getting no clear answer. He would return, he said, with press photographers and a ladder and would be photographed climbing over the wall. He was finally let in, stayed for several days, although they were the last days of his campaign, and then, according to newspaper reporters, left because of exhaustion and high blood pressure.

In an interview three years later Loftus said:

> I was told that the Friends of Medieval Dublin were told not to give me any support in the European elections; that's very serious. Now I spent four days and four nights at Wood Quay during the European campaign and I was told I was wasting my time. . . . Michael O'Leary never spent a night at Wood Quay. I was asked to stay on the site . . . because management was inflaming the workers against the occupiers, telling them that they wouldn't be paid. I talked to the workers and told them that they would get their pay. I told them that any overtime they lost I'd give them out of my environmental account.

A few days after Loftus's visit to the site, the elections were held. Loftus was defeated in his bid for the European parliament; Michael O'Leary was elected.

The elections, however, were still more than a week away when the occupiers settled in on Saturday, June 2. There was a brief alarm that day when a piece of construction equipment was brought to the site; negotiations, in which the gardai were involved, led to withdrawal of the machine. Four of John Paul's men, however, were allowed on the site to check on the pumps, which had to be kept running to prevent flooding of the north end of the site. The dogs were exercised and fed, but not allowed to run free. At three o'clock F. X. Martin held a press conference, at five o'clock a kind of executive committee of the occupiers—F. X. Martin, Richard Haworth, Leo Swan, and Bride Rosney—met to draw up a set of rules for the occupation, and later in the evening the rules were proposed to the whole body of occupiers. More visitors appeared; one was an unhappy Fianna Fail candidate for the city council who wanted his name removed from the anti–Wood Quay list which the Friends had been circulating among voters. He failed to convince the occupiers that he was not in fact anti and he stayed on the condemned list. Other visitors were the U.S. ambassador to Ireland, William V. Shannon, and his wife Elizabeth. Shannon is now University Professor at Boston University; he was head of the Washington bureau of the *New York Times* when appointed ambassador by President Carter and became extremely popular in Ireland. He dropped by the site, he said, chiefly to visit with Mary Lavin and managed to pick a time when no photographers were around. Elizabeth Shannon, who has recorded some of her reflections on Wood Quay in her book, *Up in the Park; the Diary of the Wife of the American Ambassador to Ireland*, would have gladly stayed on the site and become one of the occupiers, her husband said, if her official position had only allowed it.

Sunday, June 3, was an almost untroubled day for the occupiers, as if the spirit of the bank holiday weekend had prevailed even over protests and demonstrations. The only bane of the day was one of the construction men, who, allowed onto the site by agreement, succeeded in putting locks on all the toilets without anyone noticing what he was doing.

When Tuesday, the end of the holiday, came, fifty-four occupiers were inside the site, and other demonstrators were outside. The only plan was to obstruct work by occupying the machines, the gates, and the mobile buckets. Michael O'Brien was in charge of the machines, Richard Haworth of the gates, and Sean O'Maonigh of the buckets.

At least half the contingent inside the fence was made up of the politically and culturally prominent: Mary Lavin, James Plunkett, Tom Kinsella, Alexis Fitzgerald, Michael O'Leary, Carmencita Hederman, Sean Loftus, Denis Larkin, Gemma Hussey, and others.

When the arriving workers had collected outside the gate, Denis Larkin went out to speak to them. He tried to assure them that they would be entitled to full pay even though prevented from working, but the veteran labor leader's words did not sway the men. They went around to the Christ Church side of the gate and broke it down. The workers streamed onto the site and headed for their big hut to get equipped for work, but none of the occupiers abandoned their posts. The compressor near the main gate was almost started, but Michael O'Brien found a lever which disabled it. Although one of the bosses walked around the site exhorting the workers, a stalemate was quickly achieved, for the workers saw that the occupiers would not be moved. Tension was probably reduced by the arrival of Mike Murphy, one of Ireland's best known television personalities, a provocative and irreverent emcee and comedian. Reporters and photographers milled around the site, and in the afternoon a local teacher stopped at the gate to hand in best-wishes cards from thirty schoolchildren.

On Wednesday the sixth the confrontation between workers and occupiers was rougher than the day before. The workers broke in as they had on Tuesday; one set the pace for the attack on the occupiers by pulling one of the young women off a fence, throwing bikes and bags around, and telling the occupiers to keep "your rubbish on your side of the site." His admission that the occupiers did in fact control at least part of the site was noted with some pleasure. According to some who were watching him, he threw a barrel at Mary Lavin; at that point Richard Haworth asked the gardai to have a word with him. Mary Lavin, talking about the incident later, brushed it off, "Oh, I think somebody threw something; I don't know if anything was thrown at me." Michael O'Brien announced over the loudspeaker that one of John Paul's men was "helping the police with their inquiries into a case of assault." Laughter all around.

No sooner was law and order restored than the attention of all was caught by something happening at the crane. Dermot Walsh had seen the crane operator start up the ladder to his cab and began to race him to the top, using the framework of the tower to make his ascent. Walsh, a Donegal hotel owner with a keen interest in archaeology, had been part of the Wood Quay cause for some time; he had commissioned the Colin McIver report on Wood Quay's potential for tourism. The crane operator made it to the cab, started the engine, and began his assault on the banners erected by the demonstrators. He managed with a deft swing of the weight on the cable's end to rip the Old Dublin Society banner over the main gate and then went after the black raven, which was snatched away just in time. A worker on the ground took the cue and tore down the Liberties banner, but this was a guilt-producing act, and he later apologized to the people of the Liberties. The rescuer of the black raven was a reporter from the *Evening Herald* who lost his journalistic detachment as he watched the attack on the occupiers; after he had saved the flag he called out to those nearby to stand with him in a tent so the crane operator would not swing the weight through it. By this time, though, Dermot Walsh, still on the outside of the cab, had found a way to sabotage the crane with a peg. That was the end of the crane attack; crane operator and saboteur descended together and held a good natured postmortem on the contest. Then the water attacks began. The workers turned hoses on the occupiers on two parts of the site; in one of the instances Biddy Reid, an occupier, managed to get a hose away from a worker but came out of the struggle covered with oil. Nature seemed in league with the workers, for what had been a slight drizzle in the morning turned into a heavy downpour by eleven o'clock. The most disastrous drenching of all followed a prank by a number of the workers who climbed on top of the flat-roofed hut which the occupiers had made their kitchen, opened a hole in the roof to let in the accumulated rainwater, and inundated the food table below.

One of the workers told a reporter how he felt about the occupation:

> What do they want? I don't know what they want. That man in the dog collar over there [F. X. Martin] never did a day's work in his life. We're trying to get on with our work. Those people are long hairs. They don't want to work. They just want to waste taxpayers' money that's taken from you and me. That man wasted half a million of the taxpayers' money on those fellas with the wigs over [in] the Four Courts. For what? He lost his case and he's no intention of paying. We're going to have to pay. You and me.
> (*Irish Times*, June 7, 1979)

What if the workers were next asked to tear down Christ Church? Then, said the worker, he would be out with a placard of his own and join the demonstrators. That would be a different kind of thing altogether.

On Wednesday the sixth a treaty between the occupiers and the workers on the site was agreed on: thirty-two workers a day would be allowed on the site, the gates would be controlled by the occupiers, no machines would be used except the pumps needed for drainage, and the workers would be given jobs not entailing machinery. On Thursday the treaty was observed, but on Friday the effort to give the men contrived work just about broke down. Their reluctance to play convicts, as they put it after a day of breaking stone under the surveillance of the occupiers, was too much for even the foreman to overcome.

On Thursday June 7, the long-awaited election day, the occupiers left the site in rotation to cast their votes. The day did not end with any election news, for vote counting is a slow business in Ireland. The practice of distributing votes of losing candidates among those who stand a chance of getting elected, a consequence of the electoral system to which the name of "proportional representation" has been given, makes same-day results virtually impossible.

At Michael O'Brien's suggestion the group started its own newspaper, the *Wood Quay Occupation News*. The volunteer typist for the new organ was Jean Mattson, an American photographer and faculty member of Kean College in Union, New Jersey, who, in Dublin on a visit, had gone to Wood Quay to photograph the occupation and stayed on as one of its members. By Friday evening the paper made its appearance in a first run of fifty copies moist from a duplicating machine at Trinity College. It was snapped up by a pleased audience of occupiers who read a first-page capsulized account of their own exploits, an editorial by F. X. Martin entitled "Here We Stand" (an Augustinian just cannot shake the Lutheran style), an account by Jean Mattson of how she found Wood Quay, and some shorter features including two cartoons, one of a construction company supervisor carting Lord Mayor Paddy Belton in a mobile bucket, the latter holding aloft a sign reading "Save the Foundations of the Civic Offices."

Paddy Belton had been on the occupiers' minds during the day, as had other key candidates in the elections. Although no reports of results had yet been made, some rumors had been heard that encouraged the occupiers. Alexis Fitzgerald seemed to be doing well, as did Pat Carroll and Mary Robinson. Fianna Fail seemed to be in trouble in some unlikely areas, and there were even indications that Paddy Belton was not doing as well as expected. All of this was good news for the occupiers, or at least good rumor. Alexis Fitzgerald was willing to settle for rumor and late in the evening showed up at Wood Quay to make his acceptance speech by the light of bonfires.

With the arrival of the morning newspapers on Saturday the

hard news about the elections was out, and it was better for the Wood Quay cause than the occupiers had dared hope. The headline of the day was "Voters Sack the Lord Mayor." The defeat of Paddy Belton was a surprise. He had been an alderman, not just a councillor; he was well known, popular, a member of a political family, and, above all, he was the lord mayor. He was even a member of Fine Gael, the party that made dramatic gains in the overall election picture. "I have been ruined by women and Wood Quay," he was quoted as saying. In his place the voters elected twenty-six-year-old Mary Flaherty, who had campaigned on a pro–Wood Quay platform. She was a schoolteacher from Glasnevin who had never held public office before but who within two years would be elected to the Dáil and appointed minister of state for health and social welfare in Garret FitzGerald's coalition government. (At the same time that Mary Flaherty was made a member of the government, Alexis Fitzgerald was made lord mayor of Dublin; shortly thereafer he and Mary Flaherty were married. Wood Quay had some unforeseen effects on Dublin life.)

Perhaps the most important Wood Quay candidate to win a council seat was Mary Robinson. Her election was an occasion for celebrating among the occupiers, not merely because she and her husband were barrister and solicitor for some of them, but because as a senator she had been a vigorous defender of the archaeological work. (She was also conspicuous in the senate as a defender of women's rights, including that of easier access to contraceptives.) Her election added considerable weight to the Wood Quay forces on the council.

She holds a law degree from Trinity and has another law degree from Harvard. She has great presence before audiences. Her public voice, in fact, is often so grave and magisterial that it seems to be coming from someone other than the pretty young woman in the front of the room. Her private conversation is warm and enjoyably seasoned with irony. Her attempt to gain a seat in the Dáil in 1981 failed, probably because national issues were in the forefront of her campaign while local issues preoccupied the voters.

Because of her prominence as a political figure she got more exposure in the reporting of Wood Quay legal battles than her husband did, but both were mainstays of the activists. The two had been law students together at Trinity, but Nick Robinson had interrupted his legal training to spend a few years working as a political cartoonist in London and later in Dublin, where he was regularly featured in the *Irish Times*.

Mary Robinson was back at the site in the afternoon and addressed a meeting outside the gates at three o'clock along with F. X. Martin, Michael O'Leary, Kevin B. Nowlan, and Gemma Hussey. The only anxiety threatening the good feeling of the day was over the water which had collected at the north end of the site near the river, the largely excavated end, and which had required the installation and continuous operation of pumps; the level had been rising for two days. The body of water had been named "Sitric's Lake" by the occupiers, and now it looked like a real lake. Richard Haworth wrote a letter to John Paul about the danger the rising water posed to the city wall; a copy of the letter was sent to the director of the museum and to the acting city manager. Seamus O'Reilly, an engineer who was one of the occupiers, examined the pumps and concluded that they had been sabotaged. By Sunday the tenth the flooding of the north end had increased so much that the occupiers decided to put out a press release about it, the hand-delivered letters of the day before having brought no answers. Although Sitric's Lake made the occupiers anxious, it was a diversion. Michael O'Brien arrived with a boat which he launched on the threatening waters; it had a sail, and over the sides hung Viking shields. On Monday representatives of John Paul came to the site to examine the pumps; they had not received Richard Haworth's letter, they said.

Some aspects of the occupation had become almost routine: housekeeping, meetings, legal conferences, press releases, and visits from well-wishers. But some events took the occupiers by surprise; a reporter and photographer from the *Sunday World* arrived at the site and announced their desire to enter by kicking on the gate. Let in when they showed their press cards, they talked with some of the occupiers and went off with their story, which appeared the following Sunday under an explosively large headline, "Screw Wood Quay." With this article the *Sunday World* became the only newspaper hostile to the Wood Quay conservation effort. At the time everyone was mystified by the paper's stance; a couple of years later it was assumed that the paper's position owed something to editor Colin McClelland's connection to Sam Stephenson through McClelland's brother Bryan, an architect on Stephenson's staff. Colin McClelland denies this, saying that the paper was only reacting against massive waste of taxpayers' money paid to contractors kept idle by the archaeology: his brother's work for Stephenson Associates merely gave the paper access to drawings, cost factors, and the like, he said, but never led to pressure to influence editorial policy.

For the second issue of the *Wood Quay Occupation News* Tom Kinsella contributed a poem:

NIGHT CONFERENCE, 6 JUNE 1979

Outside the shed a drum of fiery timber
sparked and blazed in tatters of rust.
The heaped offerings of food flickered
inside, where the shadowy People were assembled.

"We have a truce. They have made
every mistake." "You couldn't trust their oath!"
An assenting growl. The tired voice rasped:
"They are not all thugs, remember. But be vigilant!"

The high cranes hung in the dark,
swift hooks and whining spider brains
locked by our mental force.
Disturbed pits and drains trickled with unease.

Where were they, with their talking done,
looking down from that window, the white cuffed
marauders, visages of rapine and arrogance,
stealthy and furious above our circle of firelight?

On the afternoon of Wednesday the thirteenth an *Evening Press*
reporter came to the site to inquire about the injunctions that had
been issued that morning against F. X. Martin and some other members of the occupation. That was the first news that anyone on the
site had that legal action, which most of the occupiers had expected
in the first few days of the occupation, was finally under way.

Just why those named in the injunction—F. X. Martin, Bride
Rosney, Seamus Kelly, Leo Swan, Paddy Healy, Seamus O'Reilly,
Richard Haworth, Michael O'Brien, and John Gallagher—were
singled out was never made clear. With the exception of John
Gallagher, the defendants selected counsel and prepared for the court
action; Gallagher refused to be represented by anyone and said that
he would not appear in court.

The high court hearing on Monday the eighteenth was before
the same Justice Gannon who had granted F. X. Martin his injunction against the corporation four months before. The case presented
by John Paul relied basically on demonstration of trespass. For the
defendants barrister Thomas Smyth argued that the court which
granted John Paul the injunction did not know that the city council
had voted on May 4 to call for a renegotiation of the contract with
John Paul. The thrust of Smyth's argument was that the likelihood
of work being stopped on the civic offices was so great that his cli-
ents were actually protecting the site from a destruction which in

the light of impending events would be gratuitous. Granting a permanent injunction against them would allow the construction work to continue for just a few days and to no end, since the most reasonable expectation at the moment was that the buildings would in fact be moved elsewhere.

Justice Gannon in his judgment stated that there were two aspects of the "incursion on the site," namely trespass and interference with the performance of contractual obligations, but that trespass had been the only one presented to the court. Earlier in the hearing he had suggested that if there were nothing to the case besides trespass, the plaintiffs had a more appropriate relief available in a suit for damages. Criticizing both sides in the case for using the court for jousting, he discharged the injunction.

The un-enjoined returned to the site for a press conference about 4:00 P.M. No fanfare, Mary Robinson had advised them, but there was much elation.

About three hours after the occupiers had settled back into tent and hut, the new city council convened for the first time. Councillor Billy Cumiskey was chosen lord mayor, a choice which was not bad news for the Wood Quay advocates, although Pat Carroll, a former member of the National Monuments Advisory Committee and a strong Wood Quay supporter, had been their first choice. At the council meeting Cumiskey proposed that no work be done on the Wood Quay site until the June 25 meeting of the council the following week, at which a motion by Mary Robinson to rescind the joint consent could be debated. Deputy City Manager Frank Feely immediately cautioned that delay in the work might render the city manager liable for surcharge, a penalty discussed at length in the following chapter and in the conclusion.

Lawyers for John Paul appealed Justice Gannon's decision to the supreme court, which began hearing the appeal at eleven o'clock on the morning of Thursday the twenty-first. After fifty minutes the court recessed for fifteen minutes, giving the defendants' lawyers time to run across the river and tell those on the site that, judging by the mood of the court, anyone left on the site in the afternoon would be jailed. A hasty evacuation was arranged, and all but John Gallagher left, carrying gear across Winetavern to be stored in the occupiers' caravan or in cars. When Richard Haworth, back in court, heard that John Gallagher was staying on the site, he broke ranks and went back to join him. Haworth's lawyer petitioned the court to be relieved of his client, and the request was granted.

The court had promised judgment for two o'clock. At that hour John Paul resumed construction work on the site. The judgment, finding in favor of John Paul and granting the interlocutory injunction, as all parties by now expected that it would, was severe in its phrasing. Chief Justice O'Higgins said:

> The facts established in the Affidavits, if adduced in a criminal prosecution would appear to establish, both the existence of a conspiracy, which is a common law offence, and a forcible entry on land which is an offence under the provisions of the Prohibition of Forcible Entry Act of 1971. All these Defendants, therefore, would seem to have incurred criminal responsibility as well as making themselves liable for damages on a massive scale. It should, therefore, be remembered by all of those so involved that their actions may render them not only criminally liable but also liable for damages which if not paid could lead to bankruptcy and a consequent blighting or disruption of careers either planned or entered upon.
>
> In these circumstances it goes without saying that it is not open to any one of the Defendants to profess that he or she is acting within the law. The contrary is manifestly the case.
>
> Such being the case it should also be noted that those who would encourage or support conduct of this kind bear a heavy responsibility. However laudable the Defendants' intentions and however meritorious their aim, an open defiance of the law cannot excuse their conduct or erase its consequences.
>
> As the law stands, the only authority entitled to determine the fate of the site is the Dublin Corporation . . .

At the meeting of the dislodged occupiers that night in the hall in John's Lane West where the whole occupation had started three weeks earlier, many of the group voiced their resentment over having been pressured into leaving the site. The decision to comply with the injunction bothered also some of the Wood Quay activists who were not at the moment part of the occupation. Two years later Eleanor Kinsella, Tom Kinsella's wife, said:

> I have a feeling that if Father Martin had allowed himself to be arrested and had been handcuffed on Wood Quay and had been marched down the hill with the cloth, Ireland would have turned, and no one would have taken Wood Quay. And I believe that he was ill advised. . . . All he had to do was the dramatic thing. He couldn't lose.

Plans were made at the meeting to get food to Richard Haworth and John Gallagher on the site. The editor of the *Wood Quay Occupation News* went off to put together issue number 3, this one to be an eight-page printed version, not typed and photocopied like the earlier two. The price had gone up from 10p. to 25p. F. X. Martin went to Keystone Studios to record the Wood Quay song by Cormac Duffy. It would be released as "F. X. and the Injunctees," he told a reporter. Not with a bang but a chorus.

10. THIS OLD JOB

ABOUT THE last year and a half of excavation on the Wood Quay site Pat Wallace said, "That was a time of just good archaeology." The most numerous and important residential finds were made during this period, and at least as much was learned about everyday life in early Dublin as had been learned in the course of all the excavations up to that point.

That last year and a half of work began in August 1979, two months after the occupation. There had been no archaeological work on the site since the first week of 1979 when F. X. Martin was granted the injunction protecting the mudbanks. Although that injunction was intended to prevent damage by the construction work on the site, the museum also stopped work at the same time that the construction work was enjoined. No one, however, paid much attention to the matter since other decisions of greater importance to the team had, independently of the museum's reaction to the injunction, brought the archaeological work to a stop: the museum had let go the archaeological workers, giving them six weeks' severance pay, and then asked Pat Wallace to tell the archaeological assistants that they were being let go as well. The assistants, unlike the workers, who belonged to the Irish Transport and General Workers Union, were not union members and were not given any severance pay. This treatment led the assistants to join the union and picket in protest against the firings. It was not until August 1979 that the museum rehired its team and began working again on the site. Another interruption in archaeological work, but a relatively short one, lay ahead in 1980, when construction workers on the civic offices went on strike; the archaeological assistants, members now of the same union as the construction workers, refused to cross their picket lines.

Pat Wallace started his team working along Fishamble Street in Viking territory north of the city wall. Ten months later, in June

1980, they had reached boulder clay and had turned up the thirteen successive levels of domestic remains that constituted the most extensive residential neighborhood found in all the excavating to date. The team then moved to an adjoining area along Fishamble immediately to the south of the first dig and excavated there until the final closing of the site in March 1981. In the relatively small area of these two digs the archaeologists found ten distinct houses and house plots rebuilt generation after generation on the same sites (but not necessarily on the same plan within each site). The perfect continuity of real estate moved down through the thirteen layers revealing furnishings and artifacts from the successive ages. All the plots were laid out to front exactly the curve of present-day Fishamble Street.

The significance of the Fishamble discoveries in the eyes of Pat Wallace is, first, what they reveal about town planning in a residential area and, second, what they reveal about house styles. In a chapter contributed to *Viking Dublin Exposed* he describes the principal form of building discovered:

> . . . a rectangular structure about 8.50m long by about 4.75m wide. The wall was usually low (about 1.25m high) and almost always of post-and-wattle construction. The roof was supported on four main posts or groups of posts arranged in a rectangle within the floor area. The large door-jambs at the almost invariable endwall entrances also appear to have played a part in supporting the roof. Hand-in-hand with this roof-support system went a three-fold subdivision of the floor space. The widest strip stretched down the middle of the floor between the endwall entrances. This was often paved, gravelled or simply consisted of mud and trampled litter. A rectangular stone-kerbed fireplace was located in the centre. Presumably, there would have been a smokehole in the roof overhead. These buildings appear never to have been provided with chimneys. Along the side walls, two areas raised of turves and brushwood formed benches which also served as beds. The buildings were of open-plan design; sometimes corner areas near the doorways were partitioned off and provided with separate entrances in order to provide greater privacy.

This kind of house, type 1 of four types in Wallace's classification of Dublin Norse structures, is the most instructive kind to compare with Viking architecture elsewhere. The lay observer would be most struck by the distinctive support system of the roofs: the four supporting posts do not stand at the corners of the house but are set well into the center of the house, holding up beams which stretch out to the point where roof and wall meet. Reconstructions of houses close to these Dublin houses have been made at other Viking sites and have now been built in Dublin in what promises to be one of the most colorful outgrowths of the Wood Quay discoveries: the Irish Life Assurance Company funded the reconstruction of a Viking village modeled on the Fishamble Street discoveries in the basement of St. Audoen's church near the Wood Quay site. The tour guides to the reconstructed village, which opened March 14, 1988, are actors in Viking costume. The project is funded for two years by Irish Life, but there is hope that if response is favorable, it may become permanent.

Reference to the Dublin Viking houses is now essential in the study of medieval Norse domestic architecture. "While sites like York, Lincoln, Durham, Lund, Sigtuna, Aarhus, Oslo, Trondheijm, Haithabu, Antwerp, etc., have shed considerable light on their respective building types and construction methods," Pat Wallace observed, "the volume of well-preserved house foundations in Dublin (especially Fishamble Street) is unparalleled except in Eastern Europe."

While the work on the Viking houses provided the archaeologists with considerable satisfaction, something going on a few feet away from the house sites left them frustrated and dismayed. By October 1980 the corporation and the architects had decided that the Viking city wall would have to come down. Its fate had been unclear from the time of its discovery; it ran through the area to be covered by the new civic offices, and it was obvious that some accommodation would have to be made on the part of the buildings or of the wall. The architect's announced plan was to leave the wall in place and make it the highlight of a museum area on the ground floors of the buildings which would rise over it. This plan provoked little enthusiasm among those interested in saving the site for two reasons: first, the conservationists almost as a reflex mistrusted any corporation plans for the site, and second, the saving of the wall in the museum area of the two buildings would have curatorial merit only—it would be of little benefit to archaeological research.

In 1978 an expensive concrete and steel base had been put under the dog-leg part of the wall and an adjacent part of the wall's west end. This structure seemed to indicate an intention on the part of the architect to keep the wall exactly in place and to accommodate the building to it. Such an intention also seems to be implicit in a story related by Bryan McClelland, the young Belfast architect on Sam Stephenson's staff mentioned in the previous chapter. McClelland, who described himself as Sam's "wall man," told of some covert treatment of the wall that, if known at the time, would have produced outraged reactions: when it was found that a part of the office building cantilevered at great expense to protect the wall would not after all clear the wall, the solution settled on was to send someone around at night to remove the top three layers of stone from the wall to make room for the obstructed beam. The anecdote, which to McClelland was a highly amusing recollection, is of interest in that it demonstrates that there was at the time a commitment on the architects' part, evidenced by the costly cantilevering, to save the wall. Even the damage done to the wall seems to have been done with anxiety.

How the decision to dismantle the wall was arrived at is not perfectly clear. Pat Russell recalls its being the result of long deliberation:

> Certain it is, however, that the proposal to dismantle part of the wall did not emerge in any sense as a sudden idea—but only after several months of careful examination and discussions involving ourselves [the corporation's Development Department], our architectural and engineering consultants and the Office of Public Works and the National Museum. There were several such meetings during the latter part of 1979 and into the early months of 1980. . . .

Pat Wallace's view of the decision was simple: "The [dismantling of the] wall was the worst thing of all that happened." The museum archaeologists were not opposed to the taking apart of the wall; they were opposed to anyone outside the museum taking it apart. There was no objection among them to eventual re-erection of the stones of the wall; Pat Wallace would have approved of re-erection if that were the favored course, but what dominated his thinking was a desire to take the wall apart in order to see how it was put together. He would have taken the Holy Grail apart if he could have put his hands on it. In an interview January 20, 1982, he said:

> In the high court in 1978 [Dermot] Kinlen made the remark on behalf of Dublin Corporation, "The wall will be preserved in its entirety." We thought then that the wall was safe. They couldn't touch it. In those days I recorded the wall. I drew the wall and photographed it. . . . I would have loved to have taken it down as an archaeologist and gone over it properly. . . . The proper way of excavating a wall like that archaeologically is to excavate in the reverse order to which it was erected. In other words, dismantle it

and see how it was built. . . . We've taken plenty of sections, but if it were excavated properly, you could tell stone for stone exactly how the wall was built, the order in which the men would have worked across the site, what side they would build from. It's very easy to do these things. I mean you can do that with the even more difficult circumstances like with wattle house building. So, you know, just careful excavation. We just couldn't do it. We were handed it in chunks.

Among the chunks that the museum was not handed was the stretch of wall core taken down near the end of the dismantling process by a bulldozer which was described in several reports as having been brought onto the site on the night of Thursday, October 30, 1980. The bulldozer's job was to clear away the core area of part of the wall on the dog-leg which had had its facing stones removed. The *Irish Times* reported that twenty yards of the wall was cleared by the machine; Matthew Byrne, whose study of the wall is discussed below, estimated that it was fifteen feet; Noel Carroll said six or seven feet. The part removed was from the stretch of wall that has been underpinned by steel beams. Pat Russell in an interview November 3, two days after the newspaper stories of the bulldozing had appeared, said:

> The impression has been given that the Wall itself has been knocked down. There was a small section of core which had been revealed by the removal of stones on the outer face of the wall last week and the bucket of the bulldozer pushed over the loose rubble of the centre core. This rubble that I am talking about is still on site at the moment and it can be archaeologically excavated.

The popular reaction to reports of the incident did nothing to weaken the contention of corporation officials that "Bulldozer is an emotional term." The dismantling operation ended with all but the Winetavern end of the wall, the part under the west office block, taken down and stored in gabons, steel net cages, on the Fishamble side of the site.

Of all those, apart from the archaeologists, who observed the wall at this time no one recorded the observations better than did Matthew Byrne, a bricklayer and stonemason from the Dublin suburb of Dun Laoghaire. Although he was employed by the Board of Works, his interest in the wall did not come from his employer's connection with it, but from his own study of it. He saw in the wall the work of his mates from a thousand years before and he felt a tie with them as if he and they were members of the same union. He

began to explain the wall to the public; in a letter to the *Irish Times*,
August 18, 1979, he wrote:

> . . . the City Wall, contrary to Corporation artists' impressions, is
> not built entirely of solid stone. The method of construction was
> such that an outside leaf and an inside leaf were built separately
> and the resultant void of about one metre across was then filled in
> with rubble and mortar.
>
> No internal bonding was attempted nor were dovetailed
> stones applied; consequently the wall is weak in relation to its
> bulk. The action of constant water seepage through the top of the
> uncapped wall and its resultant expansion during frost make the
> wall highly vulnerable to downward pressure, such as machinery
> crossing over its top, which tends to cause bulging and bursting.
> Left unprotected and exposed to the elements, the same process
> would occur naturally. Time was when the wall was buried and
> the deposits of accumulated debris on both sides of the wall acted
> as a natural buttress and so preserved the wall for many centuries.
>
> Another aspect to the construction is that at the Fishamble
> Street section of the City Wall, the method of bonding the stones
> employed by the masons was inferior; in fact, it hardly exists
> compared with other sections of the wall which are of a very high
> standard. Vertical joints are not broken alternately as they should
> be, and with the proliferation of small shallow stones, the vertical
> joints are almost one straight line. Should a stone become dis-
> lodged, therefore, the next stone has not the support to remain in
> position that it should properly command with half-bonding.

On September 25, 1980, Byrne wrote to the *Irish Times:*

> Five years ago the City Wall on both sides of St. Audoen's
> Arch at Cook Street was extensively restored as a project for Euro-
> pean Architectural Heritage Year. Such was the ignorance of what
> constituted a restored stone wall that the bonding method applied
> in the reconstructed sections had not been invented until at least
> seven centuries after the original and this was never questioned to
> this date.
>
> It was the product of the scientific 18th century where nar-
> row, non-load-bearing walls, faced on both sides and therefore sub-
> ject to the strict discipline of the plumb rule, began feverishly to
> enclose the estates and country houses of the ascendancy here in
> Ireland and as such were the precursors of modern lump labor.
> These were rubble walls but built in courses of approximately
> 1' 6" in height that allowed for a row of large stones of varying

depths to be first bedded in a line and smaller stones or pieces being then used to make up the required height of the course, the process being repeated until the total required height of the wall was attained. It was labour-saving and material saving, and allowed the mason the luxury of a fresh start on a level base every eighteen inches.

This sophistication, however, served to emphasize a visual aspect of horizontal flat lines, subduing and eliminating the growth aspect of the lines of the vertical joints. It was thus the enemy of natural building employed by the uncomplicated mind of medieval man.

It worries me that the same fate should await a dismantled wall at Wood Quay, that . . . feeling for both history and the antique may succumb to the cost-consciousness of 20th century man . . .

The criterion of an ancient wall is, therefore, that it looks ancient, that it feels ancient, that it is ancient.

On June 28, 1980, the *Irish Times* published a letter from Byrne which capsulized the prevailing sentiment about the wall more perfectly than anyone else had managed to:

As a craftsman in brick and stone for over 30 years, it baffles me why a small fortune was spent shoring up part of the City Wall at Wood Quay with concrete pillars and steel girders, and yet at the present moment a 50-foot section of the wall, part of which is in excellent state of preservation, is presently being stencilled with white-painted numbers, presumably for dismantling and re-erection.

Perhaps I may be cynical, but I am left to wonder where a mason is to be found who will faithfully and conscientiously copy and reproduce the rhythm and spontaneity of a rough and random wall that was an art form of its time.

Claiming affinity as I do with the ancient masons, and aware of the true age of even freshly quarried stone, I abhor this gimmickry of a freshly mortared and dead reproduction for the beauty, the character and the colours that are found in decay.

The stones of Dublin's ancient wall may well be numbered, but its days are as well.

A telling detail in the story of the wall is that even the museum criticized the dismantling. A few days after "John Paul's skilled tradesmen," as Frank Fallon in the corporation's public relations office described them, began taking the wall apart, the museum withdrew its observer from the site, saying it was not getting the co-operation it needed from the corporation. "The Corporation is ready to have people observe," Breandán Ó Ríordáin, now director of the National Museum, was quoted as saying, "but you have to do more if you want to know about the archaeological interest."

The wall's tribulations did not end even with the completion of the civic offices. Part of the western end of the wall, all its stones numbered, runs under an overhang of the west office building. Stones from the dismantled wall, also numbered but not yet re-erected, lie against a corner wall at the rear of the same building; some are still held in gabions, and some are heaped loose. In June 1987 Leo Swan visited the site with a group of teachers and noticed a JCB carrying a load of the stones from the old wall across the site. Returning, he photographed the wall and the heaps of loose stones, and found that some of the stones from the old wall had not been kept for restoration to their original places in the wall but had been used for landscaping in a modern low wall that ran across the lawn in line with the old wall. Noel Carroll admitted that a mistake had been made but said the situation was "retrievable."

By 1979 the city council was largely converted to the ranks of the pro–Wood Quay forces, although the Fianna Fail group remained unregenerate. From May 1979, a month before the occupation of the site, to August 1979, when the archaeologists resumed work, the fight to save the archaeological material dominated the council's business.

It is at this point that the superior armament of the city manager was brought out on parade. The chief—and really the only necessary—weapon of the city manager was the threat of surcharge. Surcharge was the penalty of personal liability of public servants for illegal or excessive expenditures of public money. This off-with-their-heads power lay in the hands of an official known as the local auditor who was authorized to assess charges against the guilty individuals. More will be said about surcharge in the conclusion, but it will be evident at once that it is one of the most intimidating powers vested in any governmental authority in western Europe.

In response to almost every motion made by the Wood Quay councillors the city manager or his deputy replied with the surcharge threat: the measures proposed would be *ultra vires* or would constitute the breaking of a contract, the liability for which would devolve on the city manager personally except when the manager called for a listing of names of those voting for the measures; when that was done, the liability would instead devolve on the councillors voting for the measures. The surcharge threat was advanced at the council meetings of May 4, June 18, June 25, July 2, July 9, and, implicitly, August 13, 1979; in most of these cases the threat was groundless and in two cases (the meetings of May 4 and August 13) defended by reasoning so specious and tortuous as to belong in *Bleak House*. Nonetheless, the mention of the word was, most of the time, as effective as displaying a cross to a vampire.

It was not effective, however, at the May 4, 1979, meeting of the council at which a motion proposed by Councillor Pat Carroll and others called on the city manager to negotiate with John Paul and Co. to end the present contract and substitute for it a new one for building on the non-monument part of the Wood Quay site. City Manager Molloy argued that this would expose him or the councillors to the threat of surcharge, but the motion passed 22 to 15. How renegotiating a contract could put one in any jeopardy is rather hard to imagine. One of the Wood Quayites remarked, "Any contract can be renegotiated except, in Ireland, the marriage contract."

Lord Mayor Billy Cumiskey's motion June 18, mentioned in the previous chapter, to delay construction work on the site one week was put down by threat of surcharge. The June 25 meeting of the council, at which surcharge was again brought up, concentrated on costs of stopping the present building and transferring the offices; a motion was passed to determine whether financial aid could be obtained from the government to cover the costs of moving the office project. Both the minister for the environment and Pearse Wyse gave the council delegation chosen to inquire about government underwriting a contemptuous brush-off and refused to meet it.

Efforts to rescind the joint consent took two approaches. When the first, a proposal to simply and unqualifiedly rescind, failed because there was no provision in law for rescission of the consent, a second, contesting the observance of the conditions of the consent, was pursued. At a special meeting of the council July 9 Mary Robinson argued that the corporation was in violation of condition C of the joint consent, namely that the museum be given "facilities to inspect and record finds of historical or archaeological interest . . . during any excavation to be carried out by the Corporation." Dundon, the law agent, replied that "if it can be shown that facilities were afforded to the National Museum, even if not availed of, there can be no question of breach of this provision." Presented in support of Dundon's opinion was a letter from Joseph Raftery: ". . . I have to state, that, at all times, the Museum has been afforded every facility on the site by the Corporation, the architects and the various contractors." Mary Robinson had presented an affidavit by Richard Haworth describing his observations on the site:

> On the afternoon of Monday 25th June 1979 I was present on the Wood Quay site when I observed a mechanical excavator being brought to the unexcavated portion of the national monument at Fishamble Street. At about 4:00 p.m. it began to dig into archaeological layers and at 4:15 p.m. I spoke to the site engineer, Mr. Bryce, and warned him that archaeological deposits were being interfered with and urged that the National Museum should be present to exercise supervision. He said that he had just informed the National Museum and when I said that work should stop until the Museum representative arrived he ignored my request and the excavation continued. The excavator encountered a massive foundation of brick and cement of recent date set down deeply into the pre-Norman layers and tried to drag it out. In so doing considerable disturbance was caused to the surrounding archaeological deposit. I explained to the driver of the machine the nature of the damage being done but was ignored. I examined the material disturbed by the excavator which was rich in organic remains characteristic of Viking deposits and picked up from part of this a sample of the organic material and two artifacts, namely part of an antler comb and a carved wooden object, which I gave to a person outside the site with a view to having the matter brought to the attention of the City Council which was due to meet that evening and with a view to transmitting the items to the safe-keeping of the National Museum. At 5:30 p.m. I again explained the position to Mr. Bryce and the site agent Mr. McWilliams and was then removed by them from the area.

(This had happened about four days after the end of the occupation when Haworth, with John Gallagher, had stayed on the site in defiance of the court orders.)

An August 20, 1979, motion by Mary Robinson to postpone execution of the joint consent was partly defused by the corporation's announcement that it was ready to consent to continuation of the archaeological excavation for seven more months, until March 31, 1980. Presented along with the announcement were two letters from Breandán Ó Ríordáin, who had just become director of the National Museum, asking permission for the archaeologists to return to the site. With the granting of this permission, the seven-month suspension of archaeological work described above came to an end, and the final year and a half of Pat Wallace's "just good archaeology" began. As that work progressed and the residential area described earlier was excavated on Fishamble Street, the council continued monitoring it, passing several motions in 1980 to protect the Fishamble digs as much as possible.

In the final days of the excavations the archaeologists unearthed objects of wood, iron, ivory, and leather, jewelry and chains, Saxon coins, skeletons, and one of the largest Viking houses yet found on the site. On March 22, 1981, Pat Wallace brought up the last shovelful of Wood Quay earth and posed with it.

Breandán Ó Ríordáin, asked how many finds from the whole medieval excavation were in the end stored in the museum's facilities, put the figure at more than a million. If one walks through the long rows of cases in the basement of the National Museum's annex in Merrion Row, where the largest number of Wood Quay finds are stored, and pulls out drawers at random, the figure does not seem exaggerated.

There is an axiom in archaeological work that at least as much time should be allotted to the writing up of a report on a dig as was taken up by the actual excavation. If the axiom applies to the medieval Dublin digs, the National Museum should be working into the next century on its report. For a while it was questionable whether there would be a report, but on September 13, 1984, Ted Nealon, minister of state for arts and culture, announced that the government had provided funds for the preparation of the work, the first volume of which appeared in 1987. This and other books related to Wood Quay are discussed in the Further Reading appendix at the end of this book.

Lingering in the courts is a lawsuit arising out of the occupation of the site. John Paul and Co. sued the nine occupiers who were named in the injunction against the occupation for £53,000, a sum which is small change for the plaintiff but not for the defendants, who would be liable for £5,900 each.

During its last two years the archaeological work continued to command the support of the general public in Ireland and of a variety of people, sometimes in official positions, outside of Ireland. Jakob Aano, chairman of the Subcommittee on the Architectural and Artistic Heritage of Europe of the Committee on Culture and Education of the Council of Europe, continued to agitate for the archaeological work; he had been instrumental in getting the Council of Europe to pass its resolution supporting the protection of the Wood Quay archaeological work in May 1979.

There is a feeling of aftermath about Wood Quay. The activists are back at their jobs, and the schoolchildren whose teachers refused to distribute the *Schools Newletter* with the corporation's presentation of the civic offices story are moving into their careers.

Dermot Walsh, one of the Wood Quay activists mentioned in earlier chapters, expresses a fear that many share, namely that in Wood Quay Dublin may have won the war and lost the peace. Walsh is afraid that the support needed for an aggressive open-ended campaign to save all medieval sites will not be forthcoming because the sense of crisis that Wood Quay generated is now past. Is anything being done to get archaeological access to the car park on the west side of Winetavern Street right across from the Wood Quay site, he asks; obviously the Viking riches there will match what was found at Wood Quay. And so of other sites.

Dublin archaeology did, in fact, come back to life between April 1985 and February 1987 when the Board of Works, under archaeologist Ann Lynch, returned to the excavation of Dublin Castle. And other sites are on various agendas for medieval archaeology in Dublin.

Medieval Dublin is getting good press in 1988, which has been declared Dublin's millennium (1988 is not a millennium of anything in Dublin—the city fathers have made millennium a movable feast). The Viking village built by Irish Life is timed to contribute to the millennial celebration, and a good deal of that celebration centers on the Viking heritage and the new light that Wood Quay has shed on that heritage. On November 6, 1987, the city manager, Frank Feely, and other corporation officials met with Anngret Sims and other people from the days of the Wood Quay struggle to discuss the possibility of a permanent Medieval Dublin Museum. While there was no prospect of corporation funding for such a museum, there was good feeling about the idea and talk of funding from other sources.

One of the formalities of the millennium is especially dramatic as a sign of new feeling about the Wood Quay experience: Lord Mayor Carmencita Hederman announced in 1988 that a newly established Millennium Conservation Award would go to F. X. Martin, Kevin B. Nowlan, and—here's a lord mayor with heart—the Casey family, the bellringers of Fishamble Street, whose house was a command post for the conspirators planning the occupation of the Wood Quay site in 1979.

The civic offices, unimpeded after March 1981 by archaeological restraints, moved ahead at full speed, which was not exactly breathtaking. Due to open in 1984, the buildings began to be occupied in October 1986 and were fully staffed by January 1987. In June 1984 City Manager Feely put their cost to date at £27,000,000.

The other two buildings in the four-building complex, the ones planned for the north end of the site, may never be built.

About a mile away from the civic offices, on the wall of the stylish Setanta Center on Nassau Street, is one of the most imaginative inscriptions ever picked for any public building anywhere; it is a scribal note from the end of Tom Kinsella's translation of the Ulster cycle epic, the *Tain Bo Cuailgne:*

> We who have copied down this story or, more accurately, fantasy
> do not credit the details of the story or fantasy. Some things in
> it are devilish lies and some poetical figments. Some seem pos-
> sible and others do not. Some are for the enjoyment of idiots.

If the committee that chose the inscription is still in session and is ready for a comparable job for the civic offices, it might pick for the wall of one of the blockish towers a text actually found on the Wood Quay site. It was left by one of the more meditative construction men, possibly a descendant of the *Tain* scribe, and was found by the occupiers of the site in June 1979 written on one of the toilet walls: "Something funny about this old job, Mac." It would be a good choice not so much because the words might take on new meaning with every passing year, but because they might have a reconciling effect among the parties to the long archaeological-political battle—assuming that a first step toward reconciliation is finding a point on which all can agree.

CONCLUSION: IT IS IF YOU WANT IT TO BE

TALKING ABOUT the worst examples of indifference or antagonism to the Wood Quay cause on the part of officials who loved to mouth the old patriotic phrases, Douglas Gageby, editor of the *Irish Times*, said, "All of this talk about heritage—it's so selective." So it is in many official and powerful circles, but the people of Ireland seem to have a more inclusive view of heritage than the elite do. If Dublin's most ancient treasures have not been demolished as completely or as quickly as they might have been, it was because of popular resistance.

Beyond the immediate, albeit partial, successes of saving the part of Dublin that they set out to save, the members of this popular resistance achieved two unforeseen results: they created new criteria for archaeological decision making in the British Isles, and they exposed and challenged some of the most unjust and self-defeating aspects of Irish local government.

Archaeology as a science has a recognized methodology: chemical tests, carbon dating, preservation techniques, aerial photography of shadowed landscapes, and so on. Those techniques, although they will be continually modified and refined and superseded, have a bit of the absolute, the contingent absolute of all scientific method. But the extremely important area of executive decision in archaeology is still formative. What precisely is the "significance" of a site? How use a limited budget? How aggressive should the science be against competing interests? Should a site be left untouched on the assumption that future generations will have developed more sophisticated research techniques and be able to do a better job than present-day researchers, or should every available site be "used" today?

This management aspect of the science has received a great deal of attention in American archaeology, especially over the last twenty years. One evidence of that attention is the large body of federal laws dealing with archaeology and the widely distributed responsibilities of federal departments and agencies for the protection of archaeological resources. Discussions, in fact, of how to treat archaeological deposits are conducted now under the rubric of "cultural resources management," usually initialized CRM, a slightly vaguefied expression coined by the National Park Service, the government agency most involved in the protection of archaeological material in the United States. The expression is intended to take in the whole management process involved in the discovery, appraisal, rescue, preservation, study, reporting, and exhibition of elements of the archaeological (and broader cultural) heritage. The stress is on the word *management.* The federal involvement is so extensive as to be overpowering at first study. It is the fruit of progressively broader decisions made during the last few decades.

The present formative stage of archaeological policy is also a period of extremely varied treatment of the world's archaeological deposits. The relativity of treatment of archaeological treasures is often the result of forces beyond anyone's control, but even when authorities can take charge of sites, results very greatly. Mexico City puts Dublin to shame; the Aztec capital of Tenochtitlan, unearthed in the heart of Mexico City, had a significance for its twelfth-century inhabitants comparable in some ways to that which Dublin had for the ninth- and tenth-century Vikings, and it came to light in a part of Mexico City which was comparable in present-day real estate value to the area of Wood Quay. Tenochtitlan was four times the size of Wood Quay, and its finds, which included seventy-eight distinct buildings, were richer than those at Wood Quay, but the sacrifice required of the Mexicans to preserve the site was also greater than any required at Wood Quay.

The Ronson ship recently found in lower Manhattan during construction work was given royal treatment in comparison with the ships found in the Norman revetments of Wood Quay; this was thanks mainly to the generosity of the developer of the land on which the ship was found. The Hohokam Indian remains in Phoenix, on the other hand, which were threatened by an interstate highway, were given just about exactly the same treatment as the Viking remains at Wood Quay.

Probably the most instructive comparison that can be made of Wood Quay is with the Viking excavations at the Coppergate site in York, Wood Quay's closest historical counterpart. What will strike most at first is the public exhibition use of the York site; opened to tours in 1984, it is nothing short of a small Viking Williamsburg, an admirable example of curatorial and educational archaeology. In that respect it is everything that Wood Quay is not. But at the same time it is not as much as Wood Quay: Peter Addyman's description, quoted earlier of the loss of 90 percent of the York site to the building interests contrasts with the embattled rescue of the Wood Quay finds.

The respect for contracts and for developers' rights of access to valuable archaeological sites is not Addyman's personal policy but the dominant policy in England in general. Richard Haworth, who was not only one of the leading Wood Quay activists but a former student of Addyman's, said shortly after work on the site finally ended in 1981 that if Wood Quay had been in England, the dig would have been ended years earlier. In England the deadline falls like a guillotine regardless of the merits of the site.

But Dublin ignored the rules and turned Wood Quay into a most curious instance of cultural resources management. Quite simply, the management of the Wood Quay archaeological campaigns was not wholly in the hands of the authorities. What the museum, the corporation, and the government did determined to some extent the course of the archaeological work, but that course was charted by other managers as well. The Wood Quay protesters not merely put pressure on the authorities, but actually forced events. Only a fraction of the finds eventually made would have been made without them: the National Museum was willing to withdraw from the site eight years before the work finally was brought to a close. One of the complaints from the museum side of the struggle was that the protesters were meddling in the work of the archaeologists; in fact, they were not meddling at all in the work of the archaeologists, but in the work of the directors of the museum: when it came to the management side of the excavations, the protesters were among the bosses. That Wood Quay even deserves to be mentioned alongside Tenochtitlan is largely the result of this meddling.

The English fear that they will lose the confidence of developers if they do not abandon sites on the day agreed; Pat Russell of the corporation's Development Department warned that that was precisely what would happen in Dublin. But suppose archaeological work does jeopardize the confidence of the builders? Is that the end of the matter? The fear of losing the confidence of builders has just a bit of the ring of the now dust-covered argument that if blacks became too militant in their pursuit of civil rights, they might lose the sympathy of moderate whites. The black response was, in effect, keep your sympathy.

At this moment in its history cultural resources management is not rich in precedents and not anxious to speak in absolutes. Some of the Wood Quay protesters may have realized this, but even if they did not appreciate the relativity of world archaeological policy, they would have pursued the same course. Their absolute was the urgency of saving Viking Dublin. Period. As it happened, this view gained them the support of archaeologists around the world, some of whom were probably dead certain that no one in their countries would fight so vigorously to save a site. But since Wood Quay happened, it has entered the register of precedents. Is this the way to save a site? It is if you want it to be.

The other unforeseen achievement of the Wood Quay protesters, the political, developed gradually and reached a high level of intensity in 1977 when the city council began to pay close attention to the fate of the site. The conflict between the pro–Wood Quay councillors and the corporation as embodied in the city manager struck observers as exceptionally intransigent. It was bound to be so because the Wood Quay initiatives in the council were a reproach to some of the most undemocratic and self-destructive aspects of Irish government. There the chief lesson of Wood Quay may lie.

Irish local government is a novelty; like British local government, which it naturally paralleled, it grew out of nineteenth-century designs to create local authorities with limited powers of self-determination. A milestone for Ireland was the Local Government (Ireland) Act of 1898 which created local elective bodies throughout the country. They were destined to be short lived because of the coming war of independence, but their fate had a good deal to do with the form of local government that has since evolved in Ireland.

Although these early local councils were forums for nationalist and patriotic expression, they did not remain in good odor after Ireland became self-governing, for the ministers of the new government, as Basil Chubb points out in his classic *The Government and Politics of Ireland* (2d ed.), were too high minded to tolerate the inefficiency and corruption which they found in the local governing bodies and moved steadily to replace what was democratic and elective in local government with the bureaucratic and appointed. Centralization of functions and surveillance of local authorities by state officials increased yearly. As early as 1925 the Local Government Act conferred on the minister for local government the power of appointing commissioners to take over the duties of local authorities, and twice in the 1920s the minister for local government acted to postpone elections in Dublin and Cork.

The introduction of the city manager system was the most dramatic and probably the most important of the reforms in local government to emerge after independence. Although a 1926 report studying the government of the Dublin area suggested the appointment of a city manager, it was the city of Cork which in 1929 was to establish the post for the first time in Ireland. Cork's choice seems to have been influenced by the example of the city manager system then in practice in the United States and by a feeling that the city manager would be a continuation of the generally respected commissioners who had been appointed to replace suspended local bodies. One year after Cork, in 1930, Dublin adopted the manager system, and by 1942 the system had spread to the counties and covered the whole country. Its early proponents felt that the manager, combined with the elected council, insured the advantages of democratic representation and stable professional administration.

An effort was made to balance the roles of the two in distinguishing between the "reserved powers" of the council and the "executive functions" of the manager. The former include adopting the budget, borrowing money, making the rate (setting local taxes), passing by-laws (local laws), disposing of corporation property, conducting elections, and attending to ceremonial matters. The executive functions include the hiring of staff, making of contracts, and conduct of the normal business of the corporation. The City and County Management (Amendment) Act of 1955 gave the councils more power over managers, e.g., prior information about all new works undertaken by the manager and the right to prohibit these works, but the common view of the manager-council relationship is that the manager holds all the best cards. Chubb emphasizes the difference between Irish city managers and their American counterparts, citing the fact that the council can neither appoint nor dismiss the manager, who is nominated by a government board known as the Local Appointments Commission; the council can suspend a manager, but only the minister for the environment can remove one.

The frustration of the council's efforts to use its Section 4 powers when Sean Loftus's April 2, 1979, motion proposed renegotiation of the civic offices contract is a striking instance of the power of the manager (abetted by the law agent) to dominate the council. It would take fancy footwork to make the average citizen, let alone a legislator, believe that there could be anything illegal about renegotiating a contract, but is was not even fancy footwork that the manager, Molloy, used. His verdict was final because the only way to challenge it was to take it to court, and how many court challenges could councillors make at their own considerable expense? The struggle between council and manager over these Wood Quay motions was an unusually hard-fought confrontation since as a rule neither side would appeal to its prerogatives as much as the manager and deputy city manager did in these cases; usually both sides are tolerant of some blurring of the difference between reserved powers and executive functions. The corporation arguments over the Wood Quay Section 4 motions stood out not merely for their flimsiness, but for their punctiliousness.

There is an oft revised and reissued little work, *Local Government in Ireland*, originally written by Patrick Joseph Meghen and now credited to its reviser, Desmond Roche, which, *mutatis patriis*, could pass for a publication of the League of Women Voters. Pithy and informative, it has as one of its purposes the education of citizens in local government in order to encourage them to stand for office. It may have encouraged a good number, for in addition to presenting the facts of local government, it projects a reasonable-sounding, and in fact pleased, confidence that the potential of the system can be realized. Without the hint of a sell, hard or soft, it manages to be almost inspiring.

Anyone who responds to it would find Neil Collins's *Local Government Managers at Work* equally or even more engaging. Collins's book, which is probably the best introduction to Irish local government, surveys local government's history in Ireland, notes its weaknesses, penetratingly studies the character of its functionaries, and concludes that the managerial system has the potential to supply exactly the kind of high-quality professional and nonpartisan administration that its early advocates sought.

But the Roche booklet's bright view of local government and Collins's trust in the potential of the managerial system are not exactly reinforced by the commentaries of Basil Chubb, Michael D. Higgins, and other critics of the real, contemporary government scene. A common view in their work is that the centralization of control in the 1920s, however nobly motivated, left the people without strong feelings about local government and without the power to secure the protection and benefits of government in the normal democratic fashions. The centralization of control furthermore turned elected officials into consumer advocates rather than legislators. The conception of the official's role shared by official and voter alike is that officials benefit their constituents by wielding influence, not by drafting laws. An American attending a Dublin city council meeting with the preconception that this body is the local legislature would quickly find the thought of legislation receding. There is some of that, but it is not what the councillors have come together for. They are at the council meeting to approve or disapprove the initiatives of the city manager and the various corporation departments. Since the city manager is the real power and since a large percentage of Dubliners would not even recognize the city manager's picture if they saw it, the people cannot be blamed for lack of strong feeling about their representatives. Chubb, criticizing the cabinet's domination of the Dáil and the senate makes an observation which he would doubtless extend by analogy to the minister for the environment's domination of local governments: "the corollary of a powerful government with a monopoly of initiative and great powers to manage is a puny parliament peopled by members who have a modest view of their functions and a poor capacity to carry them out."

One of the central government's most important incursions into local government's freedom was the 1977 decision to abolish rates on domestic property, that is, to take away from the local governments the power to tax domestic real estate. The revenue loss was to be made up by subsidies from the central government. Although the tax relief was gratifying to many of the citizens, there was widespread complaint about the local government's loss of power to control its own expenditures. It was an additional step toward the central government's assumption of all the effective powers of local government.

One may ask, is that bad? Since the population of Ireland is about the same as the population of Chicago, might not a single central authority be both efficient and fair? Such an idea, should anyone seriously entertain it, would run into obvious pragmatic objections (land area, regionalism, and variety of public services) but, more important, it would ignore the debilitating consequences of the control that the central government already does exercise.

Few things could destroy citizens' confidence in the representatives they elect more effectively than the knowledge that these representatives could be removed from office on a whim. There is some excuse for Cumann na nGaedhal dissolving the Kerry County Council in 1923 and suspending the Dublin and Cork corporations in 1924. Those were not normal times, but 1969 was certainly normal times, and Minister for Local Government Kevin Boland's suspension from office of the whole Dublin city council that year was an outrage. Boland found the council uncooperative in approving an increase in local taxes and removed all forty-five members of the council from office and replaced them with an appointed commissioner. Boland's "Removal of Members" order (a terribly apt name, taken figuratively), which kept Dublin free of elective government for more than three years, was, unfortunately, fully within the law.

The most dramatic example of the government's inordinate surveillance over local authorities is the practice of surcharge described in the previous chapter, the penalty of personal liability imposed on local officials for uses of public funds which are judged to be *ultra vires*, in excess of their authority. The obscure figure who assesses this liability, the local auditor, stood offstage during the mounting conflicts between the council and the city manager in 1979 like a hooded executioner waiting to be called in to do his duty. As was noted above his presence rarely failed to intimidate the council since councillors knew that nothing but a court case at their own expense and inconvenience, and about the results of which no plaintiff would be optimistic, could challenge an assessment of surcharge. What happened in 1979—and could happen any time—is that the city's appointed officials squelched opposition from the city's elected officials by threatening them with financial ruin. Peace of mind is one of the perks of the city manager in Ireland; most democracies cannot offer anything to match that.

The institution of the local auditor and the practice of surcharging members of local councils were inherited from British administration. Practice in England (where the functionary is known as district auditor) and Ireland are fairly similar, although years of criticism of the office of district auditor led to new legislation in England in 1972 which considerably restricted the auditors' powers: they may now concern themselves only with illegal expenditures of local authorities, not unreasonable ones; they may not impose surcharge themselves but must ask a court of law to do so; and they may not, except when directed by the secretary of state to make a special investigation, audit books of local authorities outside of London if those authorities choose to employ their own professional auditors, who, of course, cannot impose surcharge.

William A. Robson, who devotes a section of his book, *The Development of Local Government*, to the district auditor, quotes a statement of Lord Justice Fletcher Moulton on a 1908 case involving an audit of the Westminster city council:

> The true mode of securing the good management of municipal affairs is to induce the best men to take part in them and to give their services to the community in this way. . . . If those who accept [the task] are to be liable to have their conduct pronounced upon and their character and property injured, by decisions, not of any Court of Law of the country, to which they are of course amenable, but of a special tribunal consisting of an official chosen by a government department without any powers or qualifications for holding a judicial enquiry, and discharging those functions with-

out any of those securities which protect an individual before our Courts, . . . no self-respecting man will take part in municipal affairs.

It may be argued that there was need for such surveillance when local government was emerging, both in England and Ireland, in the nineteenth century, and officials were often enough inefficient and unprofessional; whether or not that contention has any merit, the level of education, general awareness, and even sophistication of the modern member of local government makes the retention of the old punitive practice of the local auditor grotesque. In any elected body anywhere there will eventually be some incompetence and corruption; they can be dealt with when they appear the same way that crime and disorder among the citizenry can be dealt with, but to put elected officials as a class under suspicion is not only unjust and dispiriting, but also simply unrealistic. Ireland and its municipalities are, by and large, well served by both their appointed and their elected officials. On retiring from the Dublin city council in 1979, Kevin Byrne, the council's *enfant terrible,* wrote to the lord mayor:

> . . . I came to the City Council five years ago with a misconception about the Corporation of Dublin's Officials. I had erroneously thought that the citizens of Dublin were badly served. My experience over my Term of Office has not only made me change my mind as to my previous opinion but I now marvel at the dedication with which all Officials of the Corporation carry out their duties, . . . often duties over and above that required by contract. In my experience the shortfalls that exist in service are usually attributable to factors outside the Corporation's sphere of influence, and more often than not as a result of decisions made at National level.
>
> . . . I have also had to change my mind in regard to the members of the political parties on the Council. I have found them, not to be the Political Hacks—as I had been used to call them in my early days on the Council—but dedicated constituency workers who worked without any financial rewards for the good of the electorate.
>
> I still believe that the decisions by the City Council on the excavations at Wood Quay and their acceptance of the motorway lines through Dublin, to be bad decisions, but bad decisions which were a matter of judgement not of dedication.

What inefficiency, laxity, or worse faults there are in local government are specific: they are to be found here or there but are not epi-

IT IS IF YOU WANT IT TO BE

demic. During the week I spent working through records in the corporation's public relations department, Noel Carroll's office, I was struck, first, by how much of that office's work was taken up with attending, ombudsman-like, to inquiries and complaints coming in from people in all parts of the city, and second, by the assiduousness with which all the citizen inquiries were pursued through department after department until firm answers were given—when that streetlight would be fixed, when the hoardings around that maintenance yard would be replaced by something not so ugly, why this or that office had changed its regular hours last week and when would they change back. And follow-up calls were made to see that the services had been provided as promised.

One of the worst things about the surcharge threat is that it infantilizes the councillors. The voice of resignation (which is despair posing as realism) will say that the habituation to the way things are done in politics has too many deep-rooted psychological supports for reasonable proposals and reasonable actions to change it. It's of a piece with gratuitous discipline in the schools and with "No, we don't accept return of merchandise because you should know your mind when you buy."

These authority fictions, psychologically complex as they may be, have at least one support which is easy to overcome: narrowness of the field of vision. One can remain a believer in the old resignation only if one unwaveringly refuses to see what the rest of the world is doing. *Securus judicat orbis terrarum*, St. Augustine said: when the whole world makes a judgment, it's a sound one. One of the corporation defenses of the National Museum was, why should we heed the comments of foreign scholars—aren't our own Irish archaeologists as good as any in the world? Maybe they are, but how does anyone find out? It is tempting to think that the narrowness of vision goes all the way back to Celtic times. Celtic society was terribly private. The self-sufficient cattle raisers, the island without towns, the church in which abbots were more powerful than bishops, all defy the principle of open society. Bishop was an uncomfortable concept because the bishop was an *epi-scopus*, someone who oversaw and therefore saw afar; an abbot did not have to see afar.

Michael D. Higgins in a chapter entitled "The Limits of Clientelism: Towards an Assessment of Irish Politics," in *Private Patronage and Public Power*, edited by Christopher Clapham (1982), sees the modern Irish elected official on the national or local level as a perpetuator of the role of the "gombeen man," the town influence broker, the man who could get things done, the man who filled the void left by the disappearance of the landlord. Higgins gives examples of elected representatives using their wiles to get advance information about government benefits such as space in council housing due to be given to people in their constituencies so that they, the representatives, could get in touch with the recipient first, before the public announcement of the assignment was made, and pretend to be solely responsible for the benefit.

There is something amusing about this politicking, especially when the citizens themselves are aware what is going on and play at the same fiction by humoring the politician. But there is not much that is funny in the substitution of such good-ol'-boy stratagems for the direct and honest exercise of rights, which a constitution guarantees. The city of Dublin uses on its official seal what is probably the most totalitarian motto adopted by any body of government anywhere: *Obedientia civium urbis felicitas*—the obedience of the citizens is the happiness of the city. The seal is set in the stone floor of the main entrance area of the Dublin city hall; walking across it one day with Noel Carroll, I asked, "That's the city motto?" "Yes," he replied with a content smile, "that's what it's all about."

If Wood Quay had not come along, it is likely that something else would have produced a comparable democratic expression, for there are too many people in Ireland who do not want the gombeen man, and who will pay the price necessary to activate the democratic machinery. And their number is growing daily. When Wood Quay came along it invariably struck most of its supporters not only as a cultural emergency but as free speech—in the profoundest way. It is hard to tell whether the debt which the Irish owe to F. X. Martin and the Friends and the great mass of defenders of Wood Quay is more a cultural one for saving the archaeological treasures or a political one for demonstrating that the country's citizens are in control of their own political destiny—or at least can be if they want to.

While I stood one day at the hatch which opens in the glass wall of the information desk in city hall, a small hinged door through which inquiries are made (now is that a symbol or not?), a short, thin man seemed to materialize next to me. I had made my request and was waiting for some documents; he made his request. Obviously a lawyer, he was asking for an obscure-sounding report. There was something about the whole business that vexed and angered him, but he was polite to the clerk behind the hatch. We had both been waiting about three minutes when his vexation had to come out: "Dean Swift said it all. There was never a people on earth more disposed to frustrate their own best interests. If there are three simple steps needed to do something, they will try to go from A to C, bypassing B, or they will try to begin at B." Pause. "And it could be such a beautiful country; and it *is* a beautiful country. Isn't it a beautiful country?"

If one may reply with the same affection and solicitude with which the question was asked, the answer is, it is if you want it to be.

FURTHER READING

THIS SELECTIVE LIST of works pertinent to the Wood Quay story is made up of titles that are of basic importance or of peculiar interest. Most of them contain bibliographies listing other works of Wood Quay interest.

G. F. Mitchell's *Archaeology and Environment in Early Dublin* (Dublin: Royal Irish Academy, 1987) is the first volume to appear in the official archaeological publications on Wood Quay. The projected series, *The Medieval Dublin Excavations, 1962–81,* will comprise twenty-five papers in an as yet undetermined number of volumes; titles will be divided into Series A: Building and Topography, Series B: Artefacts, and Series C: Environment. Funded jointly by the Royal Irish Academy and the National Museum of Ireland, the project is being edited by F. X. Martin, G. F. Mitchell, Michael Ryan, and Patrick Wallace. Wallace's "An Archaeological Bibliography of Urban Dublin, A.D. 840–1300" is scheduled to appear in the first volume in Series B.

For the general reader the most interesting book on the archaeology of the Dublin excavations will probably be Pat Wallace's *Viking and Medieval Dublin,* forthcoming from Routledge and Kegan Paul.

The most important book to date on the whole Wood Quay story is John Bradley, ed., *Viking Dublin Exposed* (Dublin: O'Brien Press, 1984). It contains essays by Breandán Ó Ríordáin, Pat Wallace, F. X. Martin, Bride Rosney, Anngret Simms, Richard Haworth, and others involved in the events of Wood Quay. Jonathan Bardon and Stephen Conlin, *Dublin: One Thousand Years of Wood Quay* (Belfast: Blackstaff, 1984) is a strikingly designed book mainly of interest for its 12" × 16" color illustrations of Wood Quay as it has looked through the centuries. Nicholas Maxwell edited *Digging Up Dublin* (Dublin: O'Brien Press, 1980), a collection of essays by five contributors treating aspects of Dublin archaeology.

The most important work on the history of Ireland is T. W. Moody, F. X. Martin, and F. J. Byrne, *A New History of Ireland* (Oxford and New York: Oxford University Press, 1976–). As of early 1988, five of the projected ten volumes have appeared: volumes 2, 3, and 4 cover the years 1169 to 1800, volume 8 is a chronology of Irish history from the beginning to 1976, and volume 9 contains maps, genealogies, and lists. Volume 1, when it appears, will cover the period from prehistoric Ireland to the Viking period. Volume 10 will contain, among other things, a bibliography.

A large number of other works on Irish history by the three editors of *A New History of Ireland* can be found in bibliographies and catalogues. The most popular is probably T. W. Moody and F. X. Martin, *The Course of Irish History* (New York: Weybright and Talley, 1967, and other editions). A few names worth noting for further reading in Irish history are Kathleen Hughes, M. and L. de Paor, Eoin MacNeill, A. J. Otway-Ruthven, and, for the history of early Irish art, Francoise Henry. Ruth Dudley Edwards's *An Atlas of Irish History* (London: Methuen, 1973) reads easily by itself or in conjunction with other history. The A. T. Lucas article, "The Plundering and Burning of Churches in Ireland, 7th to 16th Centuries," referred to in Chapter 1, is in *North Munster Studies*, edited by E. Rynne (Limerick, 1967).

For the history of Dublin one turns to the general Irish histories, to a variety of scholarly works, or to a handful of quaint antiquaries. Charles Haliday's *The Scandinavian Kingdom of Dublin*, introd. by Breandán Ó Ríordáin (Shannon: Irish Universities Press, 1969) was first published in 1881 and is best read in conjunction with more recent histories of the period. An interesting (but hard to find outside of Dublin) book on Viking and Norman Dublin is a school text put together by the Dublin Curriculum Development Unit: *Viking Settlement to Medieval Dublin* (Dublin: O'Brien Educational Press, 1978). Elgy Gillespie's *The Liberties of Dublin* (Dublin: O'Brien Press, 1977) treats the medieval Liberties, adjacent to Wood Quay, at length. Howard B. Clarke and Anngret Simms, whose work on early Dublin history and geography was described in Chapter 1, are contributors to *A New History of Ireland* and have published a number of scholarly articles, among which can be cited Howard B. Clarke, "The Topographical Development of Early Medieval Dublin," *Journal of the Royal Society of Antiquaries of Ireland* 107 (1977): 29–51, and Anngret Simms, "Medieval Dublin: A Topographical Analysis," *Irish Geography* 12 (1979): 25–41. Both articles contain extensive bibliographies. Among the work of the quaint antiquaries alluded to above one would certainly have to include J. T. Gilbert, *A History of the City of Dublin* (Dublin: Gill and Macmillan, 1978); first printed in 1861, it is a wandering and hodgepodge treatment of the city by *street*, not by date, but its anecdotal richness is hypnotic.

Two maps that grew out of the interest in Wood Quay are especially helpful to the student of medieval Dublin. Howard Clarke's *Dublin c. 840–c. 1540: The Medieval Town in the Modern City* (Dublin: Ordnance Survey, 1978) was prepared for the Friends of Medieval Dublin; it superimposes a vividly colored map of medieval Dublin on a faint map of the modern city. The other map, *Dublin c. 840– c. 1540: The Years of Medieval Growth* (Dublin: Ordnance Survey, 1977) was also prepared for the Friends of Medieval Dublin; it is black and white, illustrated, and has a text legend on the city's medieval history.

The general reader could approach Irish archaeology through E. Estyn Evans's *The Personality of Ireland: Habitat, Heritage, and History* (Cambridge: Cambridge University Press, 1973) or Peter Harbison's *The Archaeology of Ireland* (London: Bodley Head; New York: Scribner's, 1976) or almost any other book that these two authors have written. Many of the Irish archaeologists who write primarily for their professional colleagues, Michael Herity for example, are easy reading for the nonspecialist. For an understanding of cultural resources management and its place in archaeology today one may read Don D. Fowler, "Cultural Resources Management," in *Advances in Archaeological Method and Theory*, edited by Michael B. Schiffer, vol. 5 (New York: Academic Press, 1982). On dendrochronology, discussed in Chapter 1, one may read Michael G. L. Baillie, *Tree Ring Dating and Archaeology* (Chicago: University of Chicago Press, 1982).

The standard work on Irish government is Basil Chubb, *The Government and Politics of Ireland*, 2d ed. (Stanford: Stanford University Press, 1982). Neil Collins's *Local Government Managers at Work: The City and County Manager System of Local Government in the Republic of Ireland* (Dublin: Institute of Public Adminstration, 1987) is an indispensable contribution to the subject. An important study of contemporary political Ireland is Michael D. Higgins, "The Limits of Clientelism" in *Private Patronage and Public Power*, edited by Christopher Clapham (New York: St. Martin's Press, 1982). The William A. Robson book quoted in the Conclusion is *The Development of Local Government* (London: George Allen & Unwin, 1954; reprint, Westport, Conn.: Greenwood Press, 1978).

Dublin's treatment of its post-medieval heritage is vividly described in Frank McDonald, *The Destruction of Dublin* (Dublin: Gill and Macmillan, 1985).

INDEX

www.ingramcontent.com/pod-product-compliance
Ingram Content Group UK Ltd.
Pitfield, Milton Keynes, MK11 3LW, UK
UKHW042057250325
456722UK00001B/157